PRIMARY BOOKSHELF

EXPLORATIONS:
A Guide to Field Work in the Primary School

Stephen Wass

Illustrations by
Nigel Wass

Hodder & Stoughton
LONDON SYDNEY AUCKLAND TORONTO

Acknowledgments

I would like to thank all of those colleagues in education who have been prepared to share their time and ideas with me, particularly my partner in the classroom for several years, Carol Leslie, many of the best ideas are hers, and George Ennis, a headteacher, who first demonstrated to me the rewards a commitment to field study work can bring.

British Library Cataloguing in Publication Data
Wass, Stephen
  Explorations: a guide to field work in the primary
  school.
  1. Great Britain. Primary schools. Field studies
  I. Title
  372.13′8

ISBN 0 340 51288 1

First published 1990

© 1990 Stephen Wass

Typeset by Wearside Tradespools, Fulwell, Sunderland
Printed in Great Britain for the educational publishing division of Hodder and Stoughton Ltd, Mill Road, Dunton Green, Sevenoaks, Kent by Thomson Litho Ltd, East Kilbride

Contents

Preface

Now that we are in the era of a national curriculum many of the old worries about content and priorities in the curriculum have been removed; there is an expectation that much of the children's work will be based on first-hand experience and investigation. In the past there were times when one had to argue the case for field work quite strongly, now it is clear that children will gain much of their experience and many of their insights away from the classroom.

This book is written in the firm conviction that there are few things that we do in the classroom that cannot be done better out of it. It lays down guidelines about all aspects of working with children outside the immediate school premises, and covers a whole range of problems, from those concerned with working in the local environment to questions arising from planning day trips, to the challenges of residential field weeks based,

perhaps, hundreds of miles away from home. Although written mainly on the basis of work with children in the seven to eleven age range, many of the activities described can, with perhaps some reduction in scale, be successfully applied to infants.

Following some of the tragedies that have befallen school parties in recent years the accent will be very much on safety. However, a continual harping on about the dangers involved makes for rather gloomy reading so I would like to say from the very beginning that with careful planning most aspects of the environment are accessible to children in an atmosphere that is both relaxed and enjoyable. For those who remain unconvinced about the sheer pleasure and excitement of being away with children I have included an account of two particular trips, at the end of the book, to give something of a flavour as to how these things really work out in practice.

1 Introduction

The rationale

There will be many points at which the content of the national curriculum is reflected in the destination of any particular outing, for example a study of light and shadow could be undertaken through a visit to a lighthouse or a backstage tour of a local theatre; an understanding of the nature of sedimentary rocks will arise directly from a trip to a suitable cliff face or nearby quarry. However, in addition to providing coverage of specific topics called for by the national curriculum, field study also has a number of other benefits which enhance the overall quality of work in school.

In examining the environment we are giving the children an opportunity to exercise their skills in situations where real problems have to be solved, especially if they also have a hand in the planning and administration of their excursions. Many children become reluctant learners when they can see little point in what they are doing but put them on a hillside with a compass to navigate by and angles become important; present them with a large amount of factual information about the submarine they are on and note-taking flourishes; present them with a view of a waterfall they have had to spend an hour or two walking to and they will be desperate to measure its height, calculate how much water is pouring over its lip and discover what kind of rock is so soft that it can be carved by running water.

There are so many aspects of the environment that need studying that groups of children, working with their teacher, can

Figure 1.1 *The outdoor 'classroom'*

1

actually do real research; they can measure, count and record things that many adult researchers would like to examine but do not have the time or the resources to do so. A class of thirty or so children represents a tremendous reservoir of enthusiasm and energy which is often held in check by teachers. With appropriate guidance this can be released in such a way that they may discover Roman towns, record the information on rapidly decaying gravestones or plot the disappearance of species of wild flowers – all these things have been done and more. Taking the next step on from here children are rarely content with studying the environment, they see that there are things to be done too: litter to collect, ponds to dig out, community newsletters to print and circulate.

In taking children out of the classroom we are putting them in touch with authentic experiences which they can respond to in a creative way that can both extend particular skills and foster their personal development. I have seen a group of children act their way up a mountain incorporating the various features of the landscape into their unfolding narrative. Indeed, some of the best poetry I have ever read came from a late night visit to a deserted slate quarry and I have met children so wrapped up in the sketch they were doing of broken glass in an industrial landscape that they missed their lunch!

The experience of being away with a group is also a social one which can bring great enjoyment. Children who one has known only in school often behave in completely unexpected ways when away from home for an extended period. Their personalities unfold in new directions and parents frequently remark on how much more assured and self-reliant their children appear on returning home.

There is also a sense in which the study is valuable in its own right and not just as a vehicle for extending the usual classroom skills. We can all, to a greater or lesser extent 'read' our environments. Everything is where it is for a reason so that our surroundings are the product of a whole series of processes carried on through time gone by. In this country especially there is very little that can truly be described as 'natural' landscape. Some of our 'wildest' upland areas are in fact 'derelict landscapes', the result of forest clearance during the Bronze Age leading to erosion and depletion of the soil, a kind of prehistoric environmental disaster which is now happening on a larger scale to the tropical rain forests. If we can gain some understanding of the ways in which our environment has been shaped, particularly by people, then we ought to be better equipped to take part in the decision-making processes that effect the future of our world. An historical environmental perspective will not necessarily throw up a solution to every problem, but an understanding of their roots has to go some of the way towards an answer.

As well as examining the benefits for children we should also look at what the teacher gets out of it. Apart from the satisfaction of delivering parts of the curriculum in an exciting and creative way, the teacher will gain endless new insights into the ways in which the class and individuals operate. There is the pleasure of working in new and often very attractive surroundings, the challenge of organising a complex undertaking and the rewards of seeing everything come together satisfactorily. For many teachers it is their first experience of some of the management skills which go into the normal running of the school.

The locations

There are many different locations that can usefully form a venue for a school visit, indeed the opening of new museums is proceeding at a pace that has probably not been seen since the last century. Of course the facilities and support available vary widely depending on the way each particular resource is managed. There are a number of different kinds of provision that you can expect to find once you begin to explore.

Naturally there are many locations which

17th century
cottages within
medieval
boundaries

Water mill

Site of medieval
fish ponds

Motte and Bailey
castle

19th century
farm buildings

13th century
church

Ridge and furrow
– medieval fields

18th century
vicarage

16th century inn

Medieval streets
and property
boundaries

19th century
terraced housing

19th century
church

19th century
coaching inn

17th century
vicarage

19th century
weaving sheds

19th century
monument

15th century
manor house

Figure 1.2 *No matter where they are located all schools have access to an environment
that contains much of interest*

exist purely as places, so that any visit has to be self-supporting as it were. Included in this first category are the many geological features which make up the landscape – aspects of the natural environment for example, ponds and streams or areas of moor or woodland as well as the built environment consisting of the many ancient monuments marked on the maps, the churches and houses of our rural communities, the terraces and industrial remains of the large towns and cities and the modern housing estates and shopping centres. Questions of access to these areas are dealt with in the next section, but it needs to be said here that once you move off the public highway, contact with the landowner becomes of great importance.

It is easy to fall into the trap of seeing field work as something which takes place exclusively in the rural environment, but for many schools working close to home means working in urban surroundings. This is not without its difficulties: there is the ever present danger from traffic, the presence of other members of the public and a thousand and one other distractions which may prevent children from getting down to the business in hand, be it drawing a crumbling factory facade or doing a traffic count. So many problems – and yet with a landscape so rich in sites, all within easy access of most schools, it would be very sad if we turned our backs on such fertile ground for exploration purely for the sake of convenience.

In a sense other sites benefit or suffer, depending on your point of view, from the degree of packaging they are subject to. Some have little more than a carpark and ticket office, others are so heavily marketed that they have become part of something called the 'heritage' industry. There are a number of agencies responsible for maintaining sites as well as a variety of private commercial concerns.

The National Trust is one of the country's biggest landowners and has in its care many thousands of acres of land thought worthy of preserving in some way. Much of the land is open to the public all year round and car parking may be available, along with the occasional informative panel or notice. Details of the sites in their care can be found in the National Trust Handbook, available in most bookshops or else direct from The National Trust, 42 Queen Anne's Gate, London SW1H 9AS. School parties wishing to book visits can normally obtain discounts on any admission charges of up to 50 per cent, and teachers are normally allowed a free visit in order to plan their activities. The Scottish National Trust based at 5 Charlotte Square, Edinburgh EH2 4DU is responsible for properties north of the border.

In terms of access to the natural countryside the various county-based Naturalists Trusts administer areas of land chosen for their conservation value and often provide interpretative material of a very high standard. Many of them have education officers and some, such as Berkshire, Buckinghamshire and Oxfordshire Naturalists Trust (BBONT), have produced illustrated guides to their reserves. As they are not always shown on maps, the best course of action in the absence of local knowledge is to address any enquiries to the Nature Conservancy Council at Northminster House, Peterborough PE1 1UA.

English Heritage is an organisation set up by the Government to run those ancient monuments which have been taken into the care of the nation. They range in period from the Neolithic long barrow at Stoney Littleton, Avon, probably some 5000 years old, to the Stott Park Bobbin Mill, Cumbria, which went out of production in 1971. They are responsible for some of the country's best known tourist attractions such as Stonehenge and The Tower of London, as well as little known sites in remote areas which may only see a handful of visitors from one month to the next.

There are over 350 monuments to which admission is free for school parties. Some of these are open 'at any reasonable time' and are free for all. However, there are unlikely to be facilities on the site except for an explanatory notice and perhaps a parking space. Other monuments, for which a charge is normally made, have to be applied to in advance and a booking form filled in. Standard admission hours apply at most properties. Toilets are generally available on site and there are often small bookstalls where a range of authoritative and informative guidebooks can be purchased. Permission for free entry may sometimes be refused if large numbers of school groups are already expected on a particular day and the free admission rule does not apply at weekends. Full details of all the properties that are open to the public and booking forms can be obtained from: English Heritage, 15–17 Great Marlborough Street, London W1V 1AF. Similar organisations have been set up in Wales and Scotland. CADW is responsible for Welsh historic monuments and is based in Cardiff at Brunel House, 2 Fitzalan Road, CF2 1UY.

The churches are also custodians of an enormous number of historic properties, many of them set within grounds of great interest to the natural historian. The nation's churches represent an astonishingly rich collection of artefacts which are not only interesting in their own right as works of art or examples of early craftsmanship, but as monuments to the spiritual life of many generations right up to the present day. Unfortunately many churches are kept almost permanently locked, either through fear of vandalism or because one priest is having to minister to several parishes so that individual churches become disused. So, both as a matter of courtesy and organising an open door, it is important to make contact with the local priest. If there is not a local contact pinned to the church noticeboard, information can always be obtained from the diocese office. Many ministers have detailed knowledge of their own church and often make informative and entertaining guides who are used to addressing large groups of people.

On a larger scale, the country's great cathedrals are ideally set up to deal with large numbers of visitors, indeed in some cases they rely on the regular income that tourists bring in to pay their huge maintenance costs, and are generally well supplied with educational support materials. We have always

Figure 1.3 *Inner city areas offer chances to explore each other's way of life*

Figure 1.4 *Children can be encouraged to take a variety of approaches to any particular site*

tried in the past to take children along to a church service during the course of any particular study. For many it is a totally novel experience and it reminds them that a church is more than an empty masonry shell. These comments apply of course to all the different Christian denominations as well as other religions who maintain places of worship in this country. Precise attitudes towards school visits may vary but it is always worth making enquiries through leaders of local communities.

Other sites are in the care of local authorities and can include nature reserves or country parks, historic sites and, in particular, museums. The face of the museum service in this country has changed significantly over the past decade; indeed the term museum now covers almost any site where there is some attempt to preserve and/or explain a feature of interest. A new museum is said to be opening practically every week: some are controlled by various charitable trusts and operate on a non-profit making basis whilst others are run on a purely commercial basis.

There are museums for all kinds of things now, often covering quite specialist areas, for example the National Needle Museum, Redditch, The National Horse Racing Museum, Newmarket, and the National Museum of Gypsy Caravans in Pembroke. Many areas which were once centres of massive industrial growth are now busy preserving their industrial past in order to boost their economy and job prospects through tourism. Some concentrate mainly on the technology like the Abbeydale Industrial Hamlet in Sheffield whilst others, such as the Black Country Museum at Dudley, also try to preserve something of aspects of local everyday life and traditions. Actors dressed in appropriate costumes and briefed to 'inhabit the ruins' are becoming commonplace as are special events such as drama days laid on for schools.

Museums offer many different kinds of experience. Some are very controlled as at a North Wales slate mine we visited a couple of years ago. After being issued with their safety helmets the children climbed into a steeply sloping railcar and were lowered into the depths of the mine. At the bottom there was an old slate miner to greet them with a soft accent and some well chosen words on safety. They were then led through a baffling series of underground workings by carefully positioned lighting and a tape-recorded voice. At various points on the route the party halted and was treated to the sound of actors' voices reliving the experience of working underground, accompanied by suitably evocative background music. At the end of their walk they were lifted back towards the daylight, rather muddy, slightly damp and full of insights and memories.

Other sites offer rather more open-ended experiences, for example, the reconstructed site of a Roman fort in the Midlands. As it happened, through our own faults, there was nobody readily available to talk to us and little information to hand about what was going on. However, the site was an open one and we had come prepared. During the next couple of hours the children put on costumes they had made and we filmed an attack on the gateway and some of the 'soldiers' drilling. The children also collected and identified wildlife living on the fort's rampart and in its ditch. They measured the profile of the defences and made a plan of the foundations of the barrack blocks. They sketched items of military equipment in the small site museum and produced gigantic figures by dragging their feet across the gravel surface of the rebuilt cavalry training ring.

What to expect

What sort of museum will your visit take you to? If it is the sort of establishment like the fort where you have to supply your own organisation, how are you going to use the site? Are there any staff or printed resources to help you? The situation is open-ended – one of the kind that most teachers are fairly used to exploiting. On the other hand, if the children are to be lectured to, and much of what happens in modern museums is a kind of lecturing irrespective of the subtlety of the audio-visual support, what kind of message will they be taking home? In these cases one has to look at the content of the museum, much as one would assess a new book on the bookshelf, looking for accuracy, honesty and balance.

With such an enormous range of sites available for visits the problem is largely one of tracking down something that will match with one's wider curricular intentions. As has already been mentioned, the larger national organisations produce guides on what they have on offer right across the country. For the rest, invaluable sources of information are the two booklets produced each year by British Leisure Publications of East Grinstead House, East Grinstead, West Sussex RH19 IXA. These are *Historic Houses, Castles and Gardens Open to the Public* and *Museums and Galleries in Great Britain and Ireland* both of which are revised annually. There are other specialist publications which can be consulted *The Which Heritage Guide* (Consumers Association) is particularly good for its descriptions of the additional facilities available and arrangements for access, but has some inaccuracies in its historical notes. *School Visits, Tours, Outings and Holidays – A Guide*, an annual publication edited by D. Perkins and published by Domino Books, covers some of the same ground but has helpful additional sections dealing with other relevant matters whilst *Kids' Britain* produced for Pan Books by Betty Jerman lists a number of venues with children in mind. The various tourist boards produce a large amount of promotional material and can be questioned about places to visit either through their local tourist information offices or through their regional offices.

Apart from those places that exist specifically to cater for the interested visitor, there are other concerns which have other business to get on with, but which also open certain facilities to school parties. There are a number of large companies which maintain interpretative centres to illustrate the manufacture and benefits of their particular product – but remember most of their funding probably comes out of the advertising budget. Other places can sometimes be persuaded to open occasionally for an educational visit. Farmers can be particularly helpful if approached about a school visit; indeed your local branch of the National Farmers Union may have a list of those willing to open in this way. Since the Health and Safety at Work Act it has become almost impossible to take young children on tours of working industrial plants, but retailers and those in the service industries can sometimes be persuaded to play host to school parties. We have also been able to negotiate, again on a strictly 'one off' basis, entry into a number of historic properties still used as family homes. Again, a tactful approach with full explanations and detailed safeguards works wonders in opening otherwise locked doors.

Later sections in this book will look at the questions of detailed planning and organisation on the ground when visiting these sites, but the point needs to be made here that any teacher undertaking a visit to a particular location must be familiar with the place both from an educational and a safety point of view. The vast majority of sites where there is a charge for admission will waive all or part of this for teachers making preliminary visits – so go and see what is out there!

2   *Things a Teacher Ought to Know*

Training

Teachers who take it upon themselves to lead groups of children out on excursions need to have some additional skills over and above those in everyday use in the classroom. Although much of what happens out of school is an extension of classroom practice, and the same principles of good management apply in both cases, there are some extra points that teachers need to be familiar with.

First, many of the skills needed to move safely around the countryside and to make effective use of its resources are best learned in a practical setting, preferably on a course. Most local authorities run courses for teachers interested in outdoor education, although many of them tend to concentrate on the physical aspects. It is also true, however, that the providers of in-service training have become more responsive to requests from teachers for particular courses, so that if there is nothing available that appears to answer your needs, it is always worth asking for something to be set up, particularly if you can identify a group of teachers with similar needs.

It is not necessary to be a qualified mountain leader to enjoy being close to mountains, indeed if you are taking children into situations where such a qualification is essential then I would suggest that you are taking on more than is appropriate for primary aged children. Having said that, such courses can be very challenging and rewarding on a personal level and are the best way to really learn about things like map reading, moving safely over difficult country and basic first aid. There are many other outdoor sports-related qualifications which can be studied to give useful background information, but again such activities as canoeing, rock climbing and pot-holing are far better undertaken with much older children.

Maps

As maps are the basic tools for anyone wanting to find their way around the country, or indeed plan any kind of outdoor activity, we are going to look at what is available and how they may be used in some detail. We are remarkably fortunate in this country to have a standard of map cover that is difficult to beat anywhere else in the world. Of the whole range of maps printed by the Ordnance Survey, there are a number which are of special interest to those planning work out of doors and we shall look at these in detail.

First there are the 1:50 000 scale maps which replaced the old one inch to the mile series. These are known as the 'Landranger Series of Great Britain', the whole country is covered by a network of 204 maps each one covering an area 40 kilometres square. They are enormously useful for getting about the countryside by road and for getting a broad overview of an area in order to pick out features for closer study or to chart the approximate course for walks. Although footpaths are shown, it is not always easy to follow their precise line on the ground, particularly if poorly signposted. For accurate navigation across the countryside one really has to turn to the 1:25 000 scale 'Pathfinder' series. These sheets come in a variety of sizes covering areas from 10 kilometres square to 10 by 20 kilometres, to some much larger sheets which are published for some tourist areas. On these maps the positions of individual buildings are accurately recorded as are the boundaries of individual fields and the routes any footpaths take across them. Then there are those maps at a scale of 1:10 000, which can be used for plotting the results of any planning that you want to do yourself directly onto the map. Alternatively, they will give you representations of features on the ground such as prehistoric earthworks that will enable you and the children to make sense of the strange humps and bumps around you.

Most education authorities have agreements with the Ordnance Survey to permit the copying of parts of their maps for study purposes. Some of the maps seem to be rather expensive in the shops, and certainly if you need to buy a couple of Landranger maps and perhaps four or five Pathfinders the bill can be a heavy one. However, good maps are not something that should be stinted on as their careful study can save endless time on the ground.

It is worth taking time to become familiar with the conventions of these various maps so that they may be read in the way that musicians read a score or builders a plan.

There are a number of publications which give guidance on the interpretation of maps, but the best way to learn is to actually explore the countryside yourself, map in hand. An important and useful facility with Ordnance Survey maps is that they can be used to refer to particular locations through a system of grid references tied in to a 'National Grid'. Instructions for reading and writing such references are given on each map.

Rights of way

There are over 120 000 miles of footpaths open to us as well as a number of areas of open countryside to which we have access. All land however marginal or uncared for

Figure 2.1 *The two most useful Ordnance Survey Maps: the Landranger, scale 1:50 000 and the Pathfinder, scale 1:25 000. (Reproduced with the kind permission of the Ordnance Survey, © Crown Copyright.)*

belongs to someone, and much of it is the scene of intense industrial activity on the part of those who earn their living off the land. Public footpaths constitute rights of way so that we may travel across privately owned land. The idea of travelling is an important one, the footpath is a highway and one's rights over it are limited to those connected with making a journey. For example, if the path is blocked in some way you are entitled to take the shortest practicable route around the obstruction, being careful not to cause any damage. You may also remove enough of the blockage to allow yourself free passage although again you must be careful to do as little damage as possible.

If an individual, such as the owner of the land or his agent, tries to bar your way you may firmly but politely continue, but you may not exercise any force against such a person so, in practice, one usually turns back. The presence of any obstruction should be reported to the local highways authority who have a statutory duty to keep the footpaths clear. The question of livestock is a difficult one. The 1981 Wildlife and Countryside Act makes it illegal to keep a dangerous bull in a field crossed by a footpath but there are sometimes exceptions to this ruling, so it is quite possible that you may encounter young bulls or bulls together with cows or heifers. In fact crossing any field which contains cattle can prove worrying particularly if the children themselves are unfamiliar with livestock. Adequate planning should always result in an alternative route being available should you feel that either the animals or the children are likely to panic!

In Scotland there are no recognised rights of way but neither is there any law of trespass so that, on the whole, the careful walker may go practically anywhere.

Although footpaths are primarily routes for travelling you may stop to rest, or take refreshment, or enjoy the view or take a photograph, providing you and your party are not causing an obstruction. In a way this limits the amount of work you can do on the line of a footpath: sitting sketching is probably all right, stringing out a ten metre grid to count the local plant population is not such a good idea. Common sense is the key here. In addition, a landowner may ask you to leave the area if you are disturbing animals, damaging plants or crops or interfering with other people using the land.

On balance, if you plan any extensive investigation on or near private land it is best to obtain the landowner's permission – unfortunately this is sometimes a difficult process. There is no foolproof way to establish who the owner is of any given piece of land; only enquiries on the ground, asking at the post office or pub or contacting the local branch of the National Farmer's Union will help, but even then the person you are put into contact with may only be a tenant and perhaps reluctant to sanction large scale incursions of school parties onto the land. Having said this, once contact has been made with the landowner the relationship can prove an extremely fruitful one with additional facilities and information being made available.

The question of access to moorland and mountainside, beaches and foreshores and areas of common ground and ancient woodland is slightly different. Whilst footpaths only allow you to pass through the countryside, there are places where groups may move around much more freely. These include many areas where agreement exists between landowners and the local authority, areas where access has been established by custom and areas where the landowner has given permission for public use as do the National Trust and the Forestry Commission over the many acres of land they own. In some places there are privately owned country parks and nature trails but here access is often controlled and a fee may be charged.

Many areas of special interest or outstanding beauty have been designated 'National Parks'. The fact that land is included in a National Park does not give automatic right of access, but you are more likely to find marked paths and there will be more guidance as to where you can go safely. Common land, contrary to popular opinion, is not open to all; usually it is privately owned with certain individuals, the commoners, having rights to use the land in certain ways. However, some commons are owned by local authorities and are therefore set aside for public use. Beaches are owned land although many of them are in the hands of local authorities or access has been established by continual usage. The foreshore, between the lines of high and low tide, normally belongs to the Crown and there is no automatic right of access on foot, although, since there is an absolute right to use a boat upon it when it is covered in water, it is difficult for anyone to keep people off. Most canal towpaths are open as rights of way but some are not and the land actually belongs to the British Waterways Board.

The Country Code

The Country Code drawn up by the Countryside Commission is a basic guide to correct behaviour that protects the interests of all groups using the countryside. Its main points should be known, understood and applied by all staff and students engaged in field study work.

Walking

The representation of a footpath on a map is no guarantee that the particular route is a safe one to use at all times. Obviously some are impassable at certain times of the year, whilst others are dangerous because they skirt natural hazards or take you into countryside where it is easy to become lost. So, what basic guidelines can we follow to stay out of trouble when planning walks? Some authorities have tried to lay down almost mathematical formulae to the effect that no school party should venture to heights greater than 400 metres unless a person qualified in mountain leadership is present, although clearly this is a nonsense if the group is standing in a car park admiring the view surrounded by picnic tables and litter bins. The Ordnance Survey have published a set of calculations which enable a group leader to assess the difficulty of a walk on a scale from easy to very strenuous and difficult.

Common sense and experience may be the best guides but even then, accidents happen. One of the principles behind the detailed planning as set out in the next section is to assume that a serious mishap could befall any member of the party at any time, and if so

- Enjoy the countryside and respect its life and work.

- Guard against all risk of fire.

- Fasten all gates.

- Keep your dogs under close control.

- Keep to public footpaths across farm-land.

- Use gates and stiles to cross fences hedges and walls.

- Leave livestock, crops and machinery alone.

- Take your litter home.

- Help keep all water clean.

- Protect wildlife, plants and trees.

- Take special care on country roads.

- Make no unnecessary noise.

what ways out of the situation are available. Some other general guidelines are:

- Use way marked footpaths whenever possible and avoid long walks over difficult ground such as loose scree, marsh or deep sand.
- Remember that the walking will be much slower and more tiring going up or down hill.
- Never stray more than a kilometre from a well-made road and ensure there is easy access to it.
- Do not attempt to walk more than ten kilometres in a day. This is a recommended maximum when all factors are at their most favourable, between four and six kilometres is probably a more realistic target.
- Stay well away from the top and bottom of steep high rocky slopes.
- Avoid being close to deep or fast flowing water and never approach the sea in rough conditions when large waves are breaking – every now and then an extra big one comes along which can be a killer!
- Great care needs to be taken when walking groups of children along narrow country lanes. Normally, in the absence of a footpath it is best to walk on the right hand side of the road so as to face oncoming traffic. However, some lanes are very narrow and there are often blind bends so the rule has to be followed in the light of common sense. Often the sound of an approaching vehicle is the first warning one gets, so too much noise should be discouraged. Where possible adults should be given the tasks of walking in advance and to the rear of the party to give warnings to oncoming traffic.
- If there is any question about visibility, particularly if you expect to do a lot of walking in the road, then you should use fluorescent arm bands or clothing for the children. In addition, the adults at the front and rear of the party should be equipped with white and red lights respectively.

Always check the ground personally first

Further guidance about the detailed planning of a walk is given in later sections.

Navigation

Every adult in any party embarking on field work which takes them off the beaten track needs to be able to find their way using an Ordnance Survey map and its essential adjunct, a magnetic compass. By using these two together you will be able to 'set' the map, in other words position it so that it is oriented the same way as the landscape before you, you will be able to take bearings so as to identify landscape features and plot a route, and if two or more features of the landscape are visible to you on the map and on the ground then you can determine your own position accurately.

In many 'everyday' situations where there are plenty of easily identifiable landmarks, then the map can be set from observations of the surrounding countryside. This is simply done either by lining up one's location on the map with two or three recognisable points in the landscape or, if one's precise location is unknown, then any two known points on the map can be lined up with two known points on the ground. Often once the map is set in this way its relationship to the countryside becomes much clearer and users often experience the sensation of the whole thing coming to life in front of their eyes so that other features can be named and the way ahead planned.

In less hospitable country the compass becomes a necessity. The most popular range of compasses for outdoor work are manufactured by a Swedish company 'Silva'. There are a variety of models but they all feature a magnetic compass needle in a liquid damped housing, a graduated rotatable dial with orienting lines and arrow and a clear plastic baseplate which has an index mark, a travel arrow and a scale. These are reasonably robust instruments but must be protected from extremes of heat or cold. Detailed

Figure 2.2 *With experience maps can be read to build up a picture of the landscape*

instructions are included for the various methods mentioned above with which the user should become acquainted, practising initially on familiar ground. Many of these techniques can be learned alongside the children.

In the course of a country walk a combination of techniques will be used to ensure that the correct route is followed. Although direction is a vital element in navigation, distance can also be important. When examining a route on the map the distance involved can be measured using a little device called an opisometer. This has a small wheel with a milled rim which is run over the surface of the map causing a pointer to turn against a graduated scale. From this the distance, depending on the scale of the map, can be read. Less accurate methods involve laying threads of cotton along the route and then measuring the length of the threads against a ruler.

It is useful to have an awareness of the speed at which your party is walking so that some idea of distance covered can be gained by looking at the amount of time that has elapsed. This is something which can actually be measured for each group as a practical exercise, but remember that difficulties under foot and weariness can all affect the rate at which a party may be moving. As a general guide most school groups manage two to three kilometres in an hour of walking on roads or well made footpaths. As conditions deteriorate so will the rate of progress.

All these methods can be practised close to home both by the adults in the party and as a preparatory exercise by the children. Proficiency with a compass is not only a useful aid to navigation but also has several other applications in field work as we shall see later. However, it must be said that in the normal course of events correct choice of location and route, together with advance planning should render these methods unnecessary for anything apart from their educational value once out and about.

Figure 2.3 *Distances on a map can be found either with a thread or, more accurately, by opisometer*

Weather

One of the unpredictable factors that affects all outdoor activities is the weather. No matter how carefully organised a day's outing is, if the plan does not make allowances for deteriorating weather conditions then the organiser is asking for trouble. The British weather is well known for its unpredictability; days that start out sunny and dry can end with several inches of snow on the ground; fog can disappear as quickly as rain can arrive. No wonder we spend so much time talking about the weather. This variability in the weather has much to do with being on a small and complexly formed land mass where local patterns in the weather make overall forecasting difficult. However, this does not absolve the organiser of any outdoor excursion from obtaining the best information possible about local weather conditions. Apart from the national forecasts given out on television, radio and in the press, regional forecasts can be heard on local radio stations or obtained on the telephone from the local Weatherline service, and information about other local forecasts may be found in the telephone directory. It is often the practice in some of the tourist sites to post a copy of the latest forecast on local noticeboards and outside information offices. The different extremes of weather all bring risks of which we need to be aware.

Provided the children are all dressed appropriately, mild rain should not present too much of a problem. Summer rain can feel quite warm, but guard against children discarding their coats no matter how warm they feel because chill can soon follow. On days which are already cold, getting wet can increase the risk of exposure quite dramatically. Particularly difficult is being caught out in conditions of driving rain where the combination of rain blowing into the face and slippery ground underfoot can cause falls. Prolonged and heavy rain can also change the landscape so that the thin trickle you all stepped over on the way out can easily become a raging torrent on the way back; paths which have been worn down by generations of passing walkers become natural water courses once the heavens open and patches of level ground can be transformed into marshy land that slows down progress enormously.

A fall of snow, whilst it may alter the landscape and make it something magical is also one of the greatest hazards to be met with out of doors. Although bad weather seldom lasts for long, in the short term conditions can be far worse than anything seen in the Alps for example. Because the fall of snow is so unpredictable over much of the country, and some areas see a whole winter go by without anything but the slightest flurry, school parties can be caught out by the snow even if their planned excursion was well into the spring. Apart from the physical discomfort, one of the main difficulties when snow blankets the countryside is finding your way about: country which one thought was reasonably familiar becomes alien territory as landscapes are blotted out and landmarks transformed. Closer to hand the actual line of any path or trackway can disappear completely.

A strong wind has a considerable cooling effect so that impact of low temperatures on exposed parts of the body becomes increasingly severe – this is known as wind chill. The weather forecaster will often quote figures well below the general temperature to illustrate the risks of being caught unprotected in the wind. Strong headwinds will slow down the progress of a walk considerably and small children may become quite distressed by its force. Another risk is that of actually being bodily blown over to take a nasty fall or, in some tragic cases, a fatal one when the victim is carried over a cliff edge.

Mist and fog also represent hazards, poor visibility for whatever reason means problems in finding the way, difficulties in keeping a large party together, limited educational opportunities, and increased risks when walking on roads. Bad weather in general can lower everyone's spirits and make the mechanics of sketching or surveying so tiresome that in most cases it is better to abandon the attempt to work out of doors.

Figure 2.4 *As long as the children are well-equipped light rain ought not to prevent outdoor activities*

The onset of poor weather is no more than an inconvenience if it interrupts your exploration of an historic town centre, but in remote areas it can become a matter of life and death.

Even the best of weather brings its dangers. Teachers who would not dream of exposing their children to the risks associated with low temperatures will quite cheerfully parade children around on blazingly hot days when there is always the chance of sunburn, sunstroke, heat exhaustion and dehydration. Sunny weather means that sensible decisions have to be made about the amount of time spent out of doors and the kind of protective clothing it is necessary to wear.

Teachers should never be afraid to cancel or postpone a particular activity if the weather appears to be against them. Effective planning should mean that there is always a back up plan that can be put into effect should circumstances dictate. Equally, any day's programme should have measures built into it to ensure a flexible response to changing conditions. These points are covered more fully later on.

Emergency procedures and first aid

Every year many thousands of young children have rich rewarding, and above all safe, experiences of the wilder side of our environment. Occasionally accidents will happen – this is only to be expected. Very rarely are there real tragedies, but when these do occur, they are often the result of a comparatively minor accident which is handled badly. These are the cases which make the headlines, the press ask awkward questions like 'What was the ratio of supervising adults to children?' and yet again the guidelines are tightened up.

All members of a field trip party should know the procedures agreed or laid down for use in the case of emergency, and all adults with the party should have had, as a minimum, a day's first aid course provided by some recognised authority. Again, it must be stressed that prevention is far better than cure and effective planning will do much to eliminate the foreseeable hazards. Most fatalities that occur within school parties do so as a direct or indirect result of poor supervision. One adult to ten children is the absolute minimum. For educational purposes as well as safety, groups of five or six children to each adult are ideal. In any case, a school party of any size should have a minimum of three adults in attendance, so that in the case of an accident one adult can go for help or deal with the problem whilst the other two supervise the rest of the children.

Before any trip sets out it is important that certain information is readily available to all those who may be concerned with the party's welfare. Lists containing the names of all the children and adults involved, their addresses, the name of the next of kin and an emergency telephone number should be compiled and copies made available to all participating adults and the headteacher and/or the school secretary depending on who is left behind. Some local education authorities insist that further copies are lodged with their office and the local police so that in the event of a disaster parents can be contacted speedily.

It is just as important that full details of your itinerary are published and circulated. In the case of a day trip out in a coach, information about the route, a timetable and the location of the destination are all that are

necessary. However, if you are planning a long walk then your route needs spelling out in some detail, including any alternative plans and the circumstances in which they will be brought into play, and estimated times of arrival at particular points. This should be left with a responsible person at your base. If for some reason your party does not return, then this document will become the blueprint for any search which may be launched.

Once away from home every adult should know exactly who they are responsible for and when. Although only a qualified teacher can legally stand in for a parent, and so take responsibility for the whole party, other adults who have agreed to take on supervisory duties must take their jobs seriously. It is important to inform parents at an early stage of the exact arrangements that have been made regarding the supervision of their children and to get their agreements to such arrangements. Regular checks need to be made to ensure that all personnel are accounted for and if someone is missing the following steps should be taken:

1 A quick visual survey of the immediate locality should be made by the person discovering the absence. No matter how you feel remain calm and confident.
2 If not already gathered, the whole party should be assembled in one place and a full role call instituted.
3 The party should be questioned for any evidence as to the whereabouts or last known position of the missing individual.
4 The party should be held in one place and given something to do under the supervision of one or two adults whilst the others begin to search.
5 This search should be of an agreed duration depending on the location and any information received. At the end of, say, fifteen minutes the searchers should meet at some agreed spot.
6 The party leader now has the responsibility of making a decision of whether or not to summon professional help from the police

or coastguard. An adult member of the group should be sent to make contact with the relevant authorities whilst the others resume the search. When engaged in a search it is important that some way of maintaining communications between searchers be agreed. This may mean keeping within sight of each other or it may mean further meetings at agreed rendezvous points.

7 Once the police have been informed and the scope of the search widened the rest of the party's welfare must be considered so that they are brought back to 'base' as soon as possible.

8 Having seen the rest of the party safely on their way the leader of the group should normally remain on hand to liaise with other rescuers. Police advice should be taken as to at what stage the child's parents should be informed.

Experience shows that most cases of missing children are simply the result of individuals becoming absorbed in some particular feature or just generally dawdling so that the rest of the party moves on leaving them behind. Normally retracing the group's steps will lead to the missing person(s). However, it is important that all children understand clearly what they should do if they find themselves separated from the main party. The chief instruction is a simple one but subject to certain qualifications: *Stay where you are!* Clearly there should be some understanding of the need to find a safe place to await the returning search party. Everyone should be familiar with the international distress signal which is six blasts on a whistle repeated every minute. The correct response on the part of a rescuer is three whistle blasts once a minute. If a whistle is not available the same message can be conveyed by waving, flashing a mirror or torch or even striking two rocks together providing the same pattern is followed. If a child hears searchers calling they should respond but wait for the rescuers to approach them.

Of course, the situation for children who become separated from their group in built up areas is different. In this case they should be encouraged to identify and approach a suitable adult and ask for assistance. In most museums and parks there are attendants who can give assistance. Out in the wider world it is best to ask a police officer if one is available, otherwise other uniformed officials such as traffic wardens or postal workers, shop staff or any woman can be approached. Naturally the children should be equipped with the basic information about who they are, where they have come from, where they are staying and who to contact, if necessary, in writing.

It may be difficult to envisage how any well organised party operating on ground that is familiar, in reasonably good weather conditions, could get lost. Yet it does happen and the adults in the party have the responsibility for recovering the situation before any harm is done. If you are in any doubt about your location then proceed in this way:

1 As soon as you realise you are lost – stop. Do not carry on walking blindly forward in the vague hope that you must end up somewhere eventually.

2 Stay calm and confident. Gather the group together and give the children something to do, some sketching or an early lunch for example.

3 Consult with the other adults in the party. Check with the map. Try to determine the last place at which you were sure of your position. Take account of the amount of walking you have done since then to locate the general area of the map you must be in. Look around for landmarks and try to fix your position.

4 If you are still unsure of your position send an adult to retrace your steps and search for landmarks; other adults could be sent in other directions. A time limit should be set for these investigations and everyone should rejoin the group after that time and report their findings.

5 In the unlikely event of your group still being lost you have the difficult decision to

make as to whether to keep the whole party together and carry on moving in the direction that corresponds to the 'best guess' that the accompanying adults can make, or else to keep most of the party immobile in one spot while selected adults explore further afield in search of some recognisable feature or a friendly face that can offer help or advice. Factors influencing this decision include the time of day, the nature of the countryside and the weather conditions. In general the bleaker and more hazardous the country the more you should consider staying put. Providing you have not strayed too far from your published route somebody will eventually come looking for you!

The search for a missing person may result in the discovery of a casualty; alternatively a fall may occur before your eyes and, again, there is an injured person to deal with. Some general points about first aid are covered below but there are procedures which should be followed in the case of any injury that occurs when out walking away from any immediate medical help. Should an accident occur:

1 Assess the situation. Remember you have a responsibility to all members of your group; if an accident occurs ensure that everyone else moves out of danger if danger there is. In any case, where possible move the rest of the party some way off from the casualty and get them settled down under supervision.
2 Make sure the injured party is in no further danger, from falling rocks for example, and do not move serious casualties more than is absolutely necessary.
3 If it is clear that further assistance is likely to be needed send one of the adults in the party for help immediately. It is important that they have a clear picture of where they are so that they can direct emergency services straight to the spot.
4 Administer first aid.

If the casualty is unconscious but still breathing put them into the recovery position unless you suspect a spinal injury (see Figure 2.5).

If the casualty is not breathing you will need to check that the air passage is clear, then

Figure 2.5 *A casualty placed in the recovery position*

give mouth to mouth resuscitation. This technique must be learned as part of a proper training course. Remember that children's lungs have a smaller capacity than adults and adjust your breath pressure accordingly.

Check for heart beat by taking the pulse in the carotid artery at the side of the neck. If there is no pulse you will have to administer external chest compression to keep the blood circulating round the body. This will have to be combined with ventilation to maintain the flow of oxygen to the casualty's lungs. Again this technique needs to be learned and regularly practised as part of a first aid course. Remember fifteen chest compressions followed by two breaths is the recommended pattern. With children a single hand is used to compress the breast bone down about thirty millimetres.

Once the casualty starts breathing again they may be placed in the recovery position. Now try to assess the nature of any further injuries from which they may be suffering and proceed as follows:

1 If the casualty is conscious, an assessment can be made of the extent of any injuries received.
2 Any loss of blood from a wound must be controlled, the best method is to put a clean dressing over the wound and hold it in place. Should the blood continue to flow then additional dressings should be placed over the top of the first one.
3 There may be broken bones or other internal injuries – if you suspect this to be the case do not move the casualty. Equally, if you suspect that the injured person has received a severe blow to the head, they should not be moved. Send for specialist help.
4 Any injury is accompanied by a certain degree of shock and the patient will need plenty of reassurance. They will need to be kept warm, although their body temperature should not be allowed to rise above normal. A coat or bag or something similar between the patient and the ground will prevent heat loss, whilst extra coats or a blanket if available are helpful.

There are several excellent first aid books on the market which cover other aspects of injuries and their treatment which can be used as an aid to memory – but there is no substitute for proper training. All adult members of the party should have had at least one full day's training (or its equivalent) from a recognised body: either their local education authority or the Red Cross or St John's Ambulance Brigade.

Of course, most injuries that occur when out and about are of a minor nature: a fall which results in a grazed knee or a twisted ankle, a careless wave of the hand which is scratched on some thorns, or a sudden slip which may jar the spine or bump the head. If, after careful consideration, you are convinced that the injury is not severe and you can give sufficient first aid to enable the child to continue then do so, but if in doubt, it is always best to assume the worst and err on the side of caution by abandoning the activity and seeking medical aid.

There are a number of other conditions which could arise during the course of any outdoor work:

Bites and stings

Any animal bite which breaks the surface of the skin should always be treated seriously. First aid should be given for the wound and then medical advice sought. The only poisonous snake in this country is the adder. This is extremely common in some parts of the country, yet is a shy and retiring creature and will only bite if an attempt is made to pick it up or else it is stepped on. Children should be made aware of the danger and should only be allowed access to likely areas of risk in stout footwear. Should a child be bitten then one or two small puncture marks will be visible at the site of the attack with some swelling. Keep the casualty calm and restrict movement as far as possible to delay the spread of the poison, keeping the injured part below the level of the heart. Should breathing and heartbeat stop, then resuscitation will have to be started. Emergency aid should always be found as quickly as possible.

Bee and wasp stings are common summer happenings and are normally more frightening than dangerous. However, there are some individuals who have an unusually strong allergic reaction to stings and anyone who receives multiple stings may be at risk. In addition, stings within the mouth or throat should always be treated as serious. In normal cases the sting should be removed by scratcing it out with a finger nail; trying to pull the sting out often squeezes the attached poison sac forcing more venom into the wound. A cold compress will then ease the pain and reduce the swelling. In the case of an allergic reaction, multiple stinging or stinging in the mouth or throat, the casualty needs to be removed for hospital treatment as soon as possible. If the sting is inside the mouth then swelling can be reduced by rinsing the mouth with cold water. In severe cases if breathing becomes difficult the casualty should be placed in the recovery position.

Poisoning

There are some fungi, berries and seeds which are dangerous to varying degrees, as well as a number of agricultural chemicals which the children could come into contact with during their explorations. If you suspect poisoning and the child is still conscious, extract as much information from the child as you can about the origins of any substance taken in through the mouth, bearing in mind that they could become unconscious. If possible, preserve a sample of whatever they have taken to show the medical authorities. Summon medical aid as quickly as possible and monitor the patient to ensure that they are still breathing. If it becomes necessary to give mouth to mouth ventilation, wipe around the victim's mouth first to guard against becoming a victim yourself. All teachers leading parties who are out in the countryside should familiarise themselves with the main varieties of poisonous plants and should

impress on the children the importance of never introducing any substances into their mouths.

Used syringes are becoming a feature of some beaches and children should be on their guard agaist stepping on them accidentally or picking them up.

Cramp

Members of the party can be overcome with cramp whilst out walking, and the experience can be a very frightening one for children because of the intense pain that is sometimes felt. Cramp is actually an involuntary muscle contraction which the victim is then unable to relax. Treatment involves stretching the muscles, and then gently massaging the affected area. It can be associated with salt and fluid loss due to heat exhaustion or exposure, and so the circumstances should be carefully considered to minimise any further risk.

Effects of the cold – exposure, frostbite and hypothermia

It must be stressed that no well-planned excursion for primary aged children should lead them knowlingly into places where conditions are such that these difficulties are experienced. However, mistakes are made every year so these points continue to be important.

Exposure is not purely something experienced on top of a snowy mountain with a force 10 gale blowing. There are, in fact, many reported cases in the summer due to people being under-dressed and unprepared for the possible effects. The combination of a cold wind, dampness and inactivity, perhaps whilst sketching, can all lead to the following symptoms: irritability or unreasonable behaviour, clumsiness or unsteadiness, general slowing down of responses, shivering or cramp and difficulty with speech or vision. If you encounter one or more of these symptoms in members of your party then you must stop, find shelter and rest. Those suffering should be given additional warm clothing, energy rich foods and, if possible, a hot drink before returning as quickly as possible to 'base'.

In severe cases, perhaps with someone who has been injured and immobilised for a long time whilst awaiting rescue, hypothermia may have set in. Hypothermia develops when the body temperature falls below 35° C (95°F). The casualty will be pale and cold to the touch and may be shivering uncontrollably. As the condition worsens the shivering decreases as muscle coordination starts to fail and the casualty will become increasingly disorientated. Pulse and respiration rates fall and the casualty will slip into a coma. Treatment begins by stopping the victim from cooling any further by placing insulating material around the body. Naturally, urgent steps should be taken to find shelter and warmth, whilst at the same time sending for emergency assistance. Great care has to be taken not to dissipate the heat at the body's core any further; both massaging the limbs and placing them in close contact with the body add to the cooling effect and should be avoided. If the subject has stopped breathing then resuscitation may be needed but you will need to check very carefully because in some cases the breathing may be extremely shallow in which case attempts at ventilation can do great harm. If no immediate medical help is to hand then steps should be taken to gently warm the casualty by giving hot sweet drinks or, if possible, by placing well-wrapped hot water bottles against the body, not the limbs.

When the extremities become thoroughly chilled and the skin takes on a waxy white or mottled blue hue and feels hard and stiff, then frostbite has set in. The victim may be conscious of prickly pain or numbness and find the affected part difficult to move. The condition should be treated by slowly warming the affected part, preferably by direct skin to skin contact using the heat of your own body. Warmth and shelter need to be found and, once a more natural colour and some feeling has returned to the limb, it can then be further warmed by immersion in

warm water. The casualty should not be allowed any further exposure to the cold and hospital care sought in severe cases.

Effects of the heat – sunburn, sunstroke and heat exhaustion

Although few casualties are recorded amongst school parties, there is considerable suffering caused each summer through the power of the sun's rays. Admittedly, much of this is self-inflicted but this does not reduce the teacher's responsibility to make sure, by the use of sensible schedules and protective clothing, that those in care do not come to grief.

Sunburn is recognised as a reddening of exposed skin with blistering in severe cases. Because much of the damage is caused by ultra-violet light which can penetrate cloud cover, children can suffer even when there is little sun to be seen. The effects of sunburn are enhanced if the skin is wet with sweat or salt water or if there is a strong wind blowing. Treatment involves placing the victim in a cool and sheltered place and bathing the damaged parts with cold water. Medical advice should be obtained in severe cases.

Heat exhaustion occurs when excessive salt and water are lost from the body by sweating and are not replaced. Anyone so affected will appear pale, their skin will be clammy and their temperature may drop. They may experience headaches, dizziness, nausea and stomach cramps and could faint. To recover from this condition it is usually only necessary to rest the patient in a cool place and give them cold water to sip. More serious cases with persistent cramps and sickness or diarrhoea will need medical treatment as soon as possible.

Heatstroke results when the body's temperature rises beyond the point at which the normal cooling mechanisms can cope. Anybody so affected will begin by feeling dizzy and their head may ache. They may lose consciousness very quickly and will feel hot and flushed to the touch although the skin will be dry. The pulse may be racing and breathing laboured. Medical aid should always be sought in cases of heatstroke, and in the interim, measures should be taken to cool the body either by sponging with cold water or fanning to circulate cooling air.

The law

Teachers are, of course, expected at all times to exercise the standard of care that might be expected of a careful parent. Needless to say, few careful parents would attempt to take away thirty or more children for a week's holiday, so in practice teachers have to be extra careful! In fact the standard of care that one is being measured against is not the care that a child would receive within its own home, but the care any reasonable parent would show in a school situation. Apart from the obvious distress a teacher would suffer should anyone in his or her care come to grief, there are certain legal questions that are bound to follow any serious accident.

Teachers are not automatically liable for any injury that occurs to an individual in their care, rather it is a question of determining whether or not the accident resulted from some act of negligence on their part. Teachers must be able to show that through a combination of good planning and adequate supervision, they had taken reasonable steps to avoid all foreseeable dangers. The headteacher has a responsibility to check that all the adults involved in any out-of-school activity are well briefed on the safety aspects of their work and are fit persons to take such responsibility.

Should an accident occur as the result of the failings of some third party, then any claim that is to be made will be made against them and their insurers. It is also considered part of the exercise of proper care for the school to make sure that the pupils are insured in such a way that compensation would be forthcoming for any child injured by some outside agency.

If a claim were to be made by the parents of an injured child against a teacher who had been responsible for organising a particular trip, they would probably proceed against the local education authority who is responsible for the actions of its employees. Teachers are strongly advised to maintain membership of one of the various teacher trade unions, if for no other reason than the fact that they will be able to obtain the back-up of the union's experienced legal department.

Most schools are covered in one way or another by insurance taken out by their local education authority. There is some variation across the country as to what is actually covered by this insurance, particularly as it relates to school visits. It is important to check with the authority to discover the **scope** of any insurance cover. Most **provide** personal accident cover for staff **involved**, but may not cover all other adults. **Cover** for the children may be dependent on a list of forbidden activities, such as boating, being observed. Public liability insurance may be taken out to protect members of the group against claims for damages by any third party, and specialist insurance can be bought to guard against eventualities such as cancellation due to illness. Finally, if at any time parents' own cars are used to transport children, they should check with their own insurance companies that they are insured to do so.

3   Planning: The Early Stages

The great majority of school outings are for a single day and although most of the remarks in this chapter are addressed to those who have in mind the organisation of some kind of residential visit, obviously much that is said under these headings will also apply to those who are just planning a day trip.

Timing and seasonal factors

There are a number of factors which will affect decisions about the most suitable time of year for a field week. These are the pattern of the school year, the weather, and the tourist season. Unless circumstances make it unavoidable, the very beginning or the very end of term are perhaps best left alone because of difficulties with either preparation and packing or with unpacking and follow up. The precise timing within the term depends on the ratio of preparation to follow up that is intended, but the main possibilities are:

The second half of the spring term

A preliminary visit can be made during the half-term break, allowing two or three weeks of intense preparation and a similar amount of follow up time. The weather can still be quite severe in March and April so, perhaps, trips to urban centres, especially those which become overwhelmed with visitors during the height of the season, should be considered. Many museums and other places of interest are closed until after Easter but it is often possible to persuade them to open up for a party booking. This is perhaps not the most productive time for a week where the main thrust is to be aimed towards biological studies, especially if the season is late.

The first half of the summer term

Having made a preliminary visit over Easter and with the remainder of the summer term to follow up, this is quite a good choice. In May and June the weather is normally quite manageable and the worst of the tourist rush has yet to start. Going away at this time avoids some of the complications of planning around the inevitable end of summer term events such as sports days or secondary school liaison schemes.

The second half of the summer term

This has little to recommend it unless the week is intended primarily as a social one with plenty of relaxation. Many popular attractions are booked to capacity and transport and accommodation can sometimes prove difficult. On the other hand, if you have chosen a remote spot there is the opportunity to get away from it all and the chance of the best of the weather means you ought to be able to enjoy the outdoors at its best. A preliminary visit could be made either at Easter or the Whit half-term.

The first half of the autumn term

It is strange how some of the best weather comes after the schools have gone back in September. A visit towards the end of the month or early in October can make the most of this. Many places of interest are still doing business and the natural landscape can be particularly rewarding. One consideration that does need bearing in mind, however, is that you may have a class which is totally or partially new, in which case the administration during the build up the previous term can get a little complicated. Taken against

Figure 3.1 *Paths can change dramatically from season to season*

that is the fact that there can be few better ways to get to know a class, and for them to get to know each other, than going away together!

Trips away during the second half of the autumn term and the first half of the spring term really suffer in comparison because of the risk of consistently bad weather but are still possible if predominantly indoor activities are planned or if specialist help and equipment is made available for outdoor work.

Size and composition of the group

One of the key questions that gets asked whenever some tragedy overtakes a school party is that of the ratio of staff to students. All local education authorities have published figures which vary a little from place to place – one member of staff to twenty children is often quoted. However, in order to operate effectively and confidently out of school, it is my belief that one adult to ten children is an absolute maximum and it is far better to have groups of, say, six children to each adult. In this way it is possible to ensure not only maximum safety, but also that the most is made of all the educational opportunities that crop up. With such a ratio there are times when the groups can operate semi-independently so that the children do not continually feel they are part of one massive unwieldy unit. This can be particularly useful when moving about in busy streets or when trying to capture some of the tranquility of a woodland walk. At least two members of the party must be qualified teachers.

Individual circumstances vary so much that it is difficult to give hard and fast advice about where to obtain extra adult support. Consider inviting other specialist teachers who may visit your school or perhaps try turning to members of your county's advisory staff. 'Non-teaching' heads could either come along or release another teacher to join you. Ancillary staff from the school may want to come on a voluntary basis or you might even consider inviting a member of your own family!

If extra adults are drafted in who do not already know the children well, it is essential to have some time together in order to 'get acquainted'. I have always tried to organise a day trip some weeks before the main expedition to act almost as a dress rehearsal so that, as well as acting as a check on things like whether the children have got suitable outdoor clothing and footwear, it also enables me to try out my ideas regarding who goes with whom in which groups. It is easier to sort out any personality clashes in the comparatively calm atmosphere of school rather than waiting for the first day away when everyone is feeling tense. The more that the other adults in the party can be involved in the planning for the week, the greater the understanding they will have of your aims and the more they are likely to be committed to making the week a success.

In some ways the numbers and ages of the children in your party will be outside your control in that these groups tend to be self-selecting once the initial invitation to join the party has been sent out. Most schools who run a regular programme of field weeks try to build up the experience in children as they move through the school. The progression works something like this:

Infants –Day trips
Lower Juniors –Long weekends away
Upper Juniors –Full week expeditions

However, perfectly successful residential visits have been run with young children. Indeed, in some cases, first-year juniors often seem less distressed at being away from home than the older ones.

School policies vary when it comes to deciding which children should be offered trips. Normally, most day trips are organised on a class basis. However, it is sometimes the case that particular year groups from across the school may be drawn together for field week experience. A lot depends on how the school is organised, and in many large

27

primary schools it is often the practice to offer residential trips to all fourth years throughout the school, perhaps including some third years if numbers need to be bolstered. The thinking behind this is that the older ones are, on the whole, best equipped to deal with both the social and work aspects of a field week, but problems can arise. Preparation and follow up become difficult when children are drawn from a number of different classes, and it is often necessary to make complex changes to the normal routine so that groups can meet and work be done. Other problems can arise where the children may not be particularly well known by the staff supervising the trip. Some teachers have questioned the wisdom of packing most of the older children off on a trip together, top juniors are frequently the children with the biggest stores of anxiety and the greatest potential for really disruptive behaviour.

For a variety of reasons I have always tried to make the class the basic unit in the organisation of any residential trip, using a variety of methods to ensure that the whole class takes part. This has made the job of integrating the preparation and follow up into the normal work of the class far easier, as well as removing the spectre of those 'second class citizens' who have not been allowed to go and are either following a different curriculum or else a watered-down version of the one their more fortunate colleagues have been enjoying. It has meant that class groups of fourth and third year juniors have joined in together and on some occasions vertically grouped classes of seven- to eleven-year-olds have participated. Some small schools have considered field weeks beyond them because they have had insufficient numbers of older children to take part. Some have got round this by collaborating with other small schools, and some very fruitful partnerships have resulted. Others have responded in the way I have just indicated by lowering the age limit and taking, say, the whole junior department away, again with useful results.

The proportion of boys to girls taking part in any field week will, of course, be a function of the numbers in the class, but there are occasions, where for example the accommodation has fixed numbers of beds for boys and girls, when some further adjustments may need to be made. Where possible the ratio of male to female staff should reflect the numbers of children of each gender. In any case, with a mixed party there should always be one male and one female member of staff.

Parents

Any enterprise as demanding on resources and time as a study week away can only be a real success with the whole-hearted cooperation and support of the parents. This is not granted as an automatic right, but is something which has to be worked on both in the context of any given trip and as the result of a whole-school policy. The key element in ensuring their support is that one should communicate one's intentions as clearly as possible and as soon as possible. To illustrate the process, here is an account of a series of letters that accompanied the planning of a field week in North Wales and extended over a period of nine months:

Although we had been organising field weeks for several years, we had become concerned about the falling away of numbers of families interested. We thought that the chief problem was cost, particularly as it had been repeated on an annual basis with the use of hotels and hostels. As well as investigating the problem we hoped that the questionnaire element would make parents feel more involved with our early preparations (see Figure 3.2).

The results of our survey were published in the second letter, and clearly cost was a factor concerning a significant number of parents, an impression that had been confirmed by a number of personal contacts. Our plans for a cheaper stay in North Wales were still being worked on but we let the parents know something of the lines along which we were working and the progress we had made.

```
                                          The Hut,
                                            Hardwick C.P. School,
                                              Ferriston,
                                                Banbury.

                                        18th October

Dear Parents,
             Now that we have got the decorations in the hut sorted out we
are turning our thoughts ahead to next summer when we are hoping to take the
children away for another field week.  Plans have yet to be made but we feel
that the mountains of North Wales would be a good place to go.  However, we
noticed last summer that several families were clearly having second thoughts
about coming to Tenby.  Although we cannot give you any precise details about
our next visit, we wondered if you could help us by completing this question-
naire and returning it to us.
                         Yours sincerely,


                   Carol Leslie    Stephen Wass
-------------------------------------------------------------------------------
PLEASE TELL US HOW YOU FEEL BY TICKING THE RIGHT BOX

Yes, we are definitely interested in our child going to N. Wales   ☐

We are interested in a trip to N. Wales but we are worried about:  ☐

               the educational value ........................
               the cost ....................................
               our child being away from home ...............
               something else (please say what below) ........
No, we definitely do not want our child to go to N. Wales          ☐
```

Figure 3.2 *Initial information letter dated 18 October*

```
                                          The Hut,
                                            Hardwick C.P. School,
                                              Ferriston,
                                                Banbury.

                                        March 7th

Dear Parents,
             We thought we would let you have an up-dated progress report before
our forthcoming meeting to discuss the Welsh trip.  A number of details have
been confirmed over the past few days.  Firstly, the most important point, the
cost will definitely be held down to £25.  We have received confirmation from
Betws-Y-Coed that the church hall will be at our disposal for the full week
and bookings have been made with the Snowdon Mountain Railway, the North Wales
Quarrying Museum, Penmachno Woollen Mill, and Mr Pratt's railway.
             So far 24 places have been reserved but there are still spaces
available for anyone else who wishes to come.  If you have any queries about
the trip do come to the meeting on the 9th and chat to us about them.  See
you then.
                         Yours sincerely


                Carol Leslie          Stephen Wass
```

Figure 3.3 *Progress report dated 7 March*

We had been able to tie up various loose ends with regard to accommodation over the Christmas break, and were now in a position to publicise details of what we had in mind in a third letter (see Figure 3.3). We continued to inform parents of the overall progress of the project, particularly our plans to examine the facilities for ourselves over half-term.

The preliminary visit having been made, we were now in a position to go into much more detail about our plans and also to use the colour slides to convince any waverers of the merits of our chosen destination. Note how we continued to leave the door open for those who were still uncommitted. Because of the nature of the accommodation we could afford to be flexible about numbers right up to the week before we were due to leave – normally deposits have to be paid well in advance and you may not be able to be so accommodating for those who cannot make up their minds.

A hand-out formed the basis for discussion at the meeting we had with parents. The formal part of the meeting was designed to expound on the educational advantages of our week away and the way it linked in with various areas of the curriculum and our topic on transport. More domestic matters were dealt with through individual queries during the refreshments.

As soon as possible after the parents' meeting on 9 March, we followed up with a letter setting out precise details of the domestic details, as we knew from experience it was these sorts of things that caused parents and children most worry at home (see Figure 3.4). As the 'camping' element was to be done on a self-help basis we had made arrangements for items of equipment to be loaned around the class.

Finally, we sent out a note including various last minute reminders and a request for parents to fill in attached index cards with

Figure 3.4 *Follow-up letter setting out precise details of the trip dated 11 March*

relevant details including, of course, any current medication the child was taking. Of course, communication does not end once everyone has been away. There were a number of points we wanted to make and some thank yous that needed saying. Still keeping the parents involved, we also sent them a balance sheet to show how their money had been spent and to prepare them for next year's excursion!

Naturally, letters were not our only means of communication – more is probably achieved through personal contact on an everyday basis. It is unrealistic to expect parents to become involved with fund-raising activities for a field week, and then to shut them out of the school's affairs for the rest of the year. The climate in which we were working made the organisation of field trips a pleasure rather than a chore. It was a result of including parents in a whole range of decisions and plans for the class throughout the year.

Parents have always been the mainstay of almost all day outings. Most teachers recruit parents for their trips either by making personal approaches or by sending out a written invitation. Some teachers have had difficulties and have found that particular parents, perhaps those with more than their fair share of worries, have proved bigger problems than the children they were supposed to be helping take care of. Most staff know of any potential problems along these lines but it is always worth stopping to think before issuing a general invitation. It is essential that any parents who do take part in day trips attend some sort of briefing session so that they can be reminded of the kinds of standards of behaviour that are expected, the purpose of the outing in terms of the curriculum and the practical assistance they will be expected to give. Unless the adults are very well known to the children it is also worth organising some kind of initial get-together where they can meet their group and get to know their names.

The role of parents as participants in residential visits needs to be thought out more carefully. There is a degree of professionalism that has to be maintained by all adults who are working closely with children in a residential context. A particular child, for example, may soil their bed at night, others may become disturbed at being away from home, or have difficulties with the social situation of eating a communal meal. There is always the risk with parents that incidents experienced on a trip may find their way back into the community through the channel of gossip. This is not to say that teachers should be protected by a veil of secrecy from the effects of any mistakes that they make, rather that every parent should be confident that information about any personal difficulties that their child has during their schooling should be treated as confidential.

In addition, teachers who are on duty for twenty-four hours a day during the course of a study week will need some time to unwind. It is not always easy to relax and let slip the professional mask whilst parents are about. It can also, in some cases, be difficult to ensure equal treatment for all the children when one or two have their parents along. The message is that you need to know any individual parent who you may be considering asking to come along very well indeed, and be able to trust his or her discretion and good sense completely. Such parents can be found but are few and far between.

Finance and transport

Teachers on the whole make good book-keepers – class lists and registers are part of their stock in trade. However, the financial management of a week away where the budget can easily run to several thousand pounds is a complex task which needs careful handling. As it is still the case that by far the greatest percentage of the cost of any trip is borne by the parents, we should never forget whose money we are spending; the books should be properly kept and at the end of the day a statement of account and balance sheet presented to the parents. Some education authorities make this kind of formal accounting a condition of permitting any residential visit to take place. The comments in this section are mainly directed towards the needs of those organising a full week away, but the same principles apply on a smaller scale to a day trip.

Preparing a costing

At an early stage in the planning of any extended visit, some idea has to be formulated about the overall cost – only then can the figure be publicised and children recruited. The main headings under which expenditure needs to be considered are transport, accommodation (and food), admission charges and sundries.

Decisions about transport need to be made at an early stage, both to ensure that bookings are made in time and because transport costs are a major item of expenditure. There are three main options: minibus, coach or train.

For those schools fortunate enough to own or be able to borrow minibuses, the prospect of having one's own independent form of transport is an attractive one. However, some points stand further consideration. First, someone has to drive the bus and if the trip is a long one this will mean that the driver will probably not be at his or her best on arrival, or for that matter during the course of the week if other outings are planned. It makes good sense to include a number of drivers in the party but with the various regulations that govern the use of authority minibuses, this is not always possible. Secondly, do remember that a bus which has been used for a large number of short trips, to and from football matches for example, is not necessarily likely to perform well on a 150 mile marathon up the motorway. It is vital that school minibuses are well serviced in advance of any long distance trip. Thirdly, minibuses are not as comfortable as coaches on a long run and have nowhere near the storage space for luggage and other bits and pieces. You may only be having to pay fuel costs or a mileage allowance but do not forget the wear and tear on the vehicle and consequent depreciation.

The main disadvantage of coach travel can be the cost, but the advantages in terms of 'door to door' delivery and convenience are formidable. When hiring a coach the important point to bear in mind is that what you are mainly paying for is the driver and therefore an additional member of 'staff'. There is little actual difference between hiring a coach which seats fifty-six and one of the smaller models, so you may well choose to go for the larger version and the amount of space it gives you. We have on a number of occasions compared the cost of using the coach purely for the outward and homeward bound journeys as against keeping the coach with the party for the whole week. The latter option works out as a little more expensive, but not that much more and it also presents the option of having one's own transport during the course of the week. Additional costs have to be met in finding accommodation for the driver but this can usually be sorted out fairly cheaply.

Most schools tend to cultivate one or two coach companies, putting a lot of business their way and establishing a working relationship. Low cost should not be the primary concern when booking a coach, far more important is the character of the driver! A sullen bad-tempered driver can change the most exciting outing into a day of pure misery. The best way to avoid this is by giving the company with whom you book plenty of advance notice of the kind of trip you are planning, so that the work can be offered to someone who is likely to enjoy it. If you can arrange a meeting with the driver in advance of a lengthy trip you can discuss in detail points such as the preferred route, stopping places and possible excursions whilst away.

Most coach firms will quote you a flat rate for the journeys there and back. If you want additional milage this may well be charged at a fairly high rate so it is worth watching carefully to make sure that you do not run up a massive additional bill after all your calculations are complete.

Some school groups have run very

successful trips using British Rail, but there have been problems. First, of course, using the train only becomes an option if the school and destination are both reasonably close to stations. If coaches have to be used to any great extent at either end then the overall cost is bumped up, as is the level of inconvenience with repeated loadings and unloadings. The other main worry that teachers have is to do with the train arriving on time, particularly if a connection has to be made. Cost is difficult to predict; a number of factors seem to operate in relation to cheap rates for school parties but exactly which factors apply to any particular case seems to be almost at the discretion of individual counter staff. It is always worth pushing for additional reductions to any quoted price – it is surprising what kinds of special offers can emerge! Obviously it is necessary to book and pay in advance.

The great advantage of travel by rail, once you are all on board, everyone has found their seat and the train has left on time, is its sheer comfort. The children will have their own chairs and tables to work at as they watch the countryside speed by. There are few problems with travel sickness, toilets are at hand and reviving cups of coffee can be purchased by the staff.

Once the most suitable form of transport has been selected and the price determined, other costs can be taken into account. As soon as a firm decision has been made you must confirm arrangements in writing and receive written confirmation back from whichever transport company you have chosen to employ. It is useful to keep in touch with them as your plans unfold and to make sure any special requirements are notified well in advance. In the case of a trip to Wales, we had to ask for the front two rows of seats to be taken out so we could load a refrigerator!

The different factors governing choice of accommodation are dealt with later, here we are simply concerned with the financial implications. If there is to be a residential component to your trip, the choice is basically between a centre run by a local education authority, hostels run on a 'charitable' basis, centres, hostels or hotels run on a commercial basis, or 'camping' – indoors or out. In terms of cost there is surprisingly little to choose between them.

Some authorities run centres for outdoor education which are heavily subsidised and which are made available to school parties at a very cheap rate. Others insist that their facilities be made to pay for themselves and charge a rate in line with comparative private establishments. Concerns such as the Youth Hostelling Association offer some of the most attractive and competitively priced accommodation to be had and there are other hostels often run by the churches or similar organisations which can also offer cut price accommodation. Commercial field study centres tend to come in at the top of the range, as you will be paying not only for the cost of accommodation, but also for whatever additional facilities and staff they may provide. Despite their expense, some of these can prove excellent value because of the amount of additional support they provide. Increasingly over the past few years a number of hotels, seeing their normal holiday trade dwindling away, have opened their doors to school parties. Frequently there is little on offer in the way of specialist facilities but the prices can be very reasonable and there is often room for a little haggling. Outdoor camping through companies which hire out camp sites with tents already in place, or hiring one's own tents for the week can work out almost as expensive as booking permanent accommodation. Indeed, with living under canvas it is the experience you are paying for. The only really cheap option is indoor camping where a church hall or village hall is taken over for the week in exchange for a one-off payment to local funds, but these must necessarily be self-catering ventures and, therefore, food has to be budgeted for.

In many cases the provision of a field week is organised around existing accommodation that is well known by the staff and has probably been used in the past, so that the cost is a given amount that has to be worked around. However, if you have no strong preference as to where you go or are prepared to investigate a number of different sites in a particular area, then it is well worth starting to collect quotes and to compare prices. This exercise needs to be done at a very early stage as some centres become heavily booked up to a year in advance.

Some field weeks may be run without incurring any additional costs in the way of admission charges or fees for guides, especially if the centre of interest is on aspects of the natural environment or if trips are planned to sites in care of English Heritage and its sister organisations which offer free entry to parties booking in advance. However, there are many exciting attractions which could usefully form part of a programme of visits for which charges are made. Most make reductions for school groups – again, the secret is to approach them well in advance and explain what your

plans are. Discounts can range from 10 per cent to 50 per cent and there is usually some provision for adults in the supervisory capacity to be admitted free.

Amongst sundries, the organiser of a field week should bear in mind things like the cost of film, the cost of taking the children to the swimming pool or the cinema as a mid-week treat, the cost of maps, postcards, guidebooks and other educational materials and so on. Some of these may be paid for out of the children's pocket money allowance, but many teachers do not allow for items such as these and end up paying for them out of their own pockets.

Once the budget is complete in outline the total can be divided by the number of children likely to want to come and an overall cost for the week per individual arrived at. You may well find at this point that there is a minimum number of takers needed before the trip becomes financially viable. Our North Wales example is shown in Figure 3.5.

```
Betws-Y-Coed 1983

Projected Expenditure
(36 children, 6 adults)

£180.00 - Accommodation
£200.00 - Food
£390.00 - Coach
£107.30 - Snowdon Railway
£ 23.80 - Railway Museum
                 (adults free)

£901.10 - TOTAL


Projected Income

£900  - 36 x £25
£  ?  - Banbury Charities
£  ?  - PTA Funds
£  ?  - Other sources

£900+  TOTAL

                    S.W./C.L.
```

Figure 3.5 *The budget for a trip to Wales*

Collecting the money

Each school is obliged by law to keep a written statement of its policy for charging for school visits. Current guidelines make it quite clear that charges can only be levied for board and lodging, other costs must be met from voluntary contributions. The only exception to this is in the case of trips that take place outside school hours, in which case a charge may be made. Generally you will have to assess in advance the level of voluntary contributions you can expect to receive. Once parents have made a firm 'booking', it is perhaps not unreasonable to ask for some kind of 'pledge' in writing that the money will be forthcoming. The other important point is that no child should be barred from any activity because their parents will not make a voluntary contribution. Ways of making good any shortfall are considered below.

In order to budget effectively, parents need

to be given as much notice as possible of impending expenditure – the greater the expense the longer the warning. Normally if a field week during the summer term is planned I would inform parents of the likely cost as soon as possible, preferably at the start of the spring term, although I have on occasion given details of cost up to a year in advance.

Some schools prefer to leave the responsibility for putting the money together to the parents, and just collect in the full cost a couple of weeks before the excursion is due. However, there are a number of good reasons for considering implementing your own school-based savings scheme. By encouraging the children to make small regular payments into an account they can, if they wish, make a contribution to the cost of the week out of their own personal allowances. As well as establishing good habits for the future and providing some useful practical maths, we always find that children tend to appreciate more those things that they have helped pay for! Even if parents are bearing the full cost, many will find the facility to make small regular payments a useful one. Collecting monies in advance helps keep interest in the project alive, and the comparative frequency of payment gives some indication of the commitment (or lack of it) from certain families. In this way you are much less likely to be caught out by someone pulling out at the last minute. By putting the money collected into a suitable bank or building society account you can bolster your funds by earning some interest. Also, by having some cash in hand you will be in a position to cover any expenditure in advance of the trip and have money to cover any deposits that are required.

The mechanisms of any savings scheme will vary from school to school. I have tended to involve parents and children as much as possible but the overall responsibility for banking and managing the funds must stay with the teacher. A system that we have found to work involves preparing a class register where the amount of any weekly payments can be recorded against the child's name, and individual savings cards on which monies paid in can be listed with the date. This serves both as a record for the child and family and also as a receipt for cash taken in. To prevent money coming in in dribs and drabs and having a lot of cash on the premises during the week, we opened for business every Friday morning before school. When the books were closed for the day the column was totalled up and the amount checked against the money collected. This was then handed to the school secretary who banked it as part of the normal Friday routine. You may prefer to keep all trip monies in a separate account, both for ease of management and possible interest payments, but unfortunately some local authorities insist that all such transactions must go through the school fund or a special purposes account.

One of the periodic difficulties that needs

Expenditure

Date	Item	Amount
18/3/83	Snowdon Mountain Rly (cheque drawn on Bldg Soc.)	25-00
18/3/83	Penmachno Woollen Mill (cash to SW in exchange for cheque)	3-60
15/4/83	Oak Cash & Carry (cash)	78-58
20/4/83	Papers (cash)	7-37
20/4/83	Oak Cash & Carry (cash)	21-23
22/4/83	Papers (cash)	12-44
22/4/83	Papers (cash)	4-37
22/4/83	Wyncolls (cash)	13-08
22/4/83	Banbury School (Photocopy)	9-86
23/4/83	Valle Crucis Abbey (c)	8-82
24/4/83	Rail Museum (ch.)	22-80
25/4/83	Mountain Rly (ch.)	88-00

Figure 3.6 *A page from an account book*

very careful handling arises with those families who, for one reason or another, are unable to make the voluntary contributions called for. There are a number of ways these kinds of problems can be approached depending on the circumstances. The period over which contributions are collected can be extended so that although the family are paying the full cost, it is spread over a longer period of time – perhaps extending some months after the trip has been completed. Some families have been able to find funds for themselves from the various support agencies that operate, but usually we have covered the cost ourselves, either from general school funds, grants from the PTA, monies raised from a 'Support our Field Week' fund-raising event or from outside sources contacted by the school (see 'Other sources of income'). In these cases we have found ways to enable the children to make payments into the account to preserve the sense that everyone is contributing.

Some kind of policy decision will need to be made about the position of parents who decide to pull out at the last minute. Clearly, if you have had to use some of your funds to pay a deposit then the individuals concerned must be prepared to lose that deposit, although the legal position of those trying to claim back a voluntary contribution remains unclear. If you have not undertaken any great prior financial commitment you may feel more disposed towards offering refunds, depending on the circumstances. However, whatever you decide you must make the 'rules' clear from an early stage.

Pocket money

One of the potential sources of trouble, once away, lies with any other money the children may have with them. A lot of extra cash floating around the group can be a worry either because it gets lost or else spent on items which are not in the best interests of the company! If all the children's needs are catered for by careful planning, the only additional expenditure they will need to make will be on guidebooks, postcards or other souvenirs of places visited, or else on small presents to take home. You may choose to allow some spending on refreshments of various kinds.

We have always found it useful to control and monitor children's pocket money despite the extra labour involved. We always give parents precise guidance as to the amount of pocket money permitted, usually up to a maximum figure of, say, £5 for a full week away. This is then collected and kept in a separate cash box and a proportion of it handed out on request at the beginning of each day. Some teachers have found it useful to have access to an individual's funds in this way so that they can extract a contribution should any payment for damage be required, but I am not altogether sure of the legality of this. If you do choose to let the children hang on to their own money, it is worth making absolutely clear that you will accept no responsibility for it should it go missing.

Other sources of income

Schools have always had to involve themselves in fund-raising activities of various kinds, generally asking for money from the same people, the parents, in a variety of different guises. However, there are other sources of income which I feel schools will increasingly be drawing on in the future. The concerns from which such funds may be available fall into two categories: the charitable and the commercial. In approaching any sort of organisation, there are a number of basic points that you should bear in mind. Make your request as precise as you can, state exactly how much money is needed and what it is wanted for, if there is likely to be any useful publicity have it ready to offer and if you are putting together a package of support from different sources explain to your contact who is giving what. On the basis that 'charity begins at home' investigate what is available locally first.

There are many charitable bodies, some of

them specifically educational in their outlook and a few, even, concentrating specifically on aspects of the environment and its study. An up-to-date list of such organisations and their addresses can be found in the *Educational Grants Directory* published by Directory of Social Change. Many small communities have educational charities dating back several hundred years which were once responsible for funding the schools in a village or town. Their trustees will be local people who may well listen to any request for funds with interest. In most towns, members of the business community come together in fund-raising bodies such as Rotary Clubs, Round Tables and Lions, and we have always found them very approachable in individual cases of hardship.

Links with local companies often involve some sort of sponsorship deal so that their contribution comes from their advertising budget and you may be obliged to court publicity rather more than you might choose. Sometimes companies can be very helpful by donating help in kind, such as foodstuffs if you are self-catering, or by giving prizes that can be converted into cash by holding a draw. Whoever you choose to approach, the most important thing is to build up personal contacts well in advance of any request for help.

How to spend money

Everyone is good at spending money but there are a number of points that should be made to whoever is holding the purse-strings on a school trip. The ideal is to conduct as few cash transactions as possible whilst away. If you have been operating through an established school account you may have a cheque book with you, but the chances are you will not, in which case you will have to hand over cash and be faced with the worry of carrying it around or of keeping it in an insecure place. Alternatively, you will have to have some of the money paid into your personal account and use your own cheque book – a risky business, partly because it lays you open to suggestions of financial abuse, but mainly because you may well find yourself overspending with little prospect of getting the money back again. So, whenever possible, it is advisable to pay in advance or to get people to invoice you back at school. Providing some sort of agreement is reached in advance this is usually quite straight forward and acceptable. Having said this, there are always occasions when this is not possible or when the expenditure, on films or guidebooks for example, is so small that a cash transaction is really the only option. In these cases it is important to obtain a written receipt for presentation when the final accounts are worked out. Some kind of petty cash book needs to be kept to record this kind of spending.

Balancing the books

When the trip is all over, you have a responsibility to give some account to the parents as to how their money has been used. Also, in most authorities you will have to be able to produce the documentation for the school's own auditing to take place. A simple sheet showing sources and amounts of income and receipted items of expenditure should be sufficient. Hopefully the two should balance, usually with the addition of a small amount of cash in hand or the recording of a small loss. In the first case any remaining funds could be ploughed back into general school spending or perhaps, more satisfactorily, held over to get the next trip off to a flying start. On one exceptional occasion, parents were given a refund after part of a programme had to be cancelled and a less expensive option substituted. If the enterprise has been well planned you should not really expect to find yourself in the red. However, I have heard of parties who have been detained by unexpected changes in the weather or by industrial action and who have had to spend extra sums. The prudent manager will have a contingency fund to cover such emergencies but most school trips work on such tight budgets that this is rarely possible. The answer is not to accept personal liability, but to ask for any accounts to be settled through the school and throw yourself on the mercy of the headteacher, governors and parents when you get back!

HARDWICK SCHOOL BETWS-Y-COED ACCOUNT   BALANCE SHEET

INCOME		EXPENDITURE	
Children's subs	912-50	Coach hire	465-00
Teachers' subs	75-00	Hall hire	180-00
PTA donation	33-00	Food	254-16
Banbury Charities	50-00	Snowdon Mtn Rlwy	113-00
		Valle Crucis Abbey	8-82
		Rlwy Museum	22-80
		Swimming Pool	10-20
		Woollen Mill	3-60
		Printing workbooks	9-86
		Cash in hand	3-06
TOTAL	1070-50	TOTAL	1070-50

Please note: This is a simplified version of the full account which will not be completed until the end of the month. Anyone wishing fuller details should contact us.

S.W./C.L.

Figure 3.7 *The final balance sheet*

4 Planning: The Later Stages

Getting around

Whether you are planning a day visit to a busy town centre or a week on an isolated nature reserve you will have to plan carefully to enable your party to move about safely and effectively. The planning of detailed routes for walking during the course of an outing begins as a map-reading exercise. The details are later checked by consultation with local experts and finally, by getting your feet muddy. If you have a series of objectives in mind arising out of whatever themes you have chosen to study, then inspection of the 1:50 000 Ordnance Survey map will usually throw up several possibilities. Further study of any particular route must be made either on the larger scale 1:25 000 maps, which show sufficient detail to enable the line of a footpath in relation, say, to the boundary of a field to be picked out, or on a street plan which will give details of parking places and one-way streets.

Certain basic principles should be observed when choosing a route in the countryside. School trips with primary-aged children are not occasions for blazing trails across unknown country. Normally, well-established footpaths and bridle-ways are perfectly adequate for making your way about the British countryside. By sticking to public rights of way and being reasonably careful not to wander too far off the beaten track, the worst perils of the open countryside can be avoided, not least the risk of trespassing – there are few experiences more humiliating than being turned off a patch of ground by an irate landowner when you have a large party of children and parents in tow.

The distance walked during the course of a day's outing depends on a variety of factors including the type of country, the weather conditions, the number of stops, the nature of other activities planned, and the age and abilities of the children. It is important to remember that the pace of any group is the pace of its slowest member and that even simple operations like climbing over a stile, can slow a party down significantly, especially if it is a large one. I have already suggested that a sensible maximum distance, when all factors are at their most favourable, would be ten kilometres. The distance attempted should, of course, be far less if conditions are poor. Indeed it is important that a system of 'escape routes' is built in to any walk to take account of the possibilities of bad weather, illness or injury and fatigue.

Some 'theoretical' examples will clarify a few of the points that have to be considered in determining any given route. First, consider the planned walk outlined in Figure 4.1

This is a poor choice of route for a number of reasons. The most serious defect lies in the lack of any easy way to retreat from trouble, should the need arise. The most hazardous part of the trip must surely be the crossing of the steep-sided rocky stream valley, and should someone slip on a stone in crossing and receive a ducking, there is nothing to do but press on. Worse, if a fall on the rocks results in a broken limb a major rescue will have to be launched to evacuate the casualty. On a less dramatic note, should it start to rain, always a possibility in our climate, then there is no alternative but to complete the planned programme. Although misery of this kind may be held to be 'character building', in some circumstances it should play no part in primary school field work.

This route also suffers from other major defects. Although on the map, and perhaps even on the ground, a straight line may seem

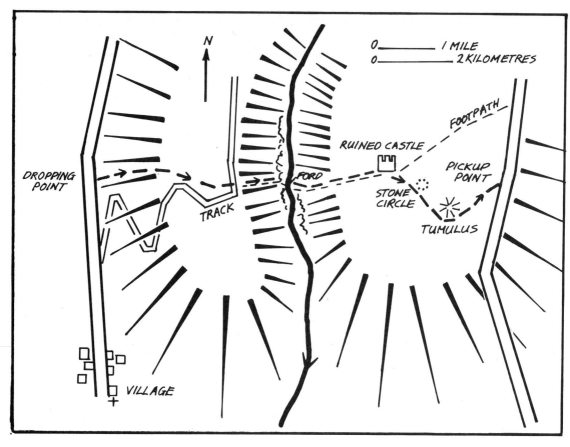

Figure 4.1 *A poor choice of route with many areas unsuitable for exploration by children*

the shortest distance between two points, old tracks and footpaths frequently represent the best choice of route. Many of these tracks have evolved over long periods of time to provide optimum conditions for the traveller. The path that snakes up the side of a steep hill makes for a far better paced climb with a gentler overall gradient than one which tackles the slope head on. The path that meanders over apparently featureless moorland may be avoiding hidden patches of marsh, whilst the track that runs just below the crest of a ridge probably affords protection from the prevailing winds.

The first few kilometres includes a lot of walking across comparatively featureless moorland. For children travelling at a slower pace, too much open ground can easily prove tedious despite magnificent views. The stops

that had been planned were to look at a group of sites clustered together towards the end of the day's walk when the children would be beginning to feel tired. It would have been far better to have picked a route where the stops were equally spaced, so that the children's interest would be held throughout the day and where there was always a reasonably immediate objective to their walking. Finally, if it is envisaged that the walk should end at some point where the party is to be picked up by a coach or minibus, it is far better that the place chosen should have some amenities and shelter available to the waiting group. If not, and the coach is delayed for any reason, the party can only loiter miserably by the roadside, totally out of touch until someone comes along.

Figure 4.2 illustrates an ideal day's

walking. The most testing and potentially hazardous part of the excursion, climbing the sides of the steep rocky valley, is tackled early on while everyone is fresh and alert. Should someone slip and break an ankle there is a track down to the main road from which help can be brought. Most of the walk is along existing footpaths and minor roads, places of interest are well spaced along the route and, most important of all, there are a number of 'bolt holes' for use should plans have to be changed. Indeed, not only should planning allow for the day's activities to be brought to a premature end should circumstances dictate, but also effective planning should provide a number of alternative routes so that the pattern of the day can be changed, depending on circumstances.

As I have already mentioned, one of the essential precautions that must be taken before setting off on any journey is to leave details of your route and estimated time of arrival with a responsible person who will know what action to take should you be delayed. When running a programme into which a number of alternatives are built it is important to itemise those choices together with some indication of factors which will govern their selection. Then, whenever possible, try and get to a phone to inform those who are monitoring your progress of any changes you make.

Coastal walking can be very rewarding although it has its own particular hazards. The first subject that has to be thoroughly mastered is that of the timing of the tides, and any walk must be planned in close conjunction with the relevant tide-tables and

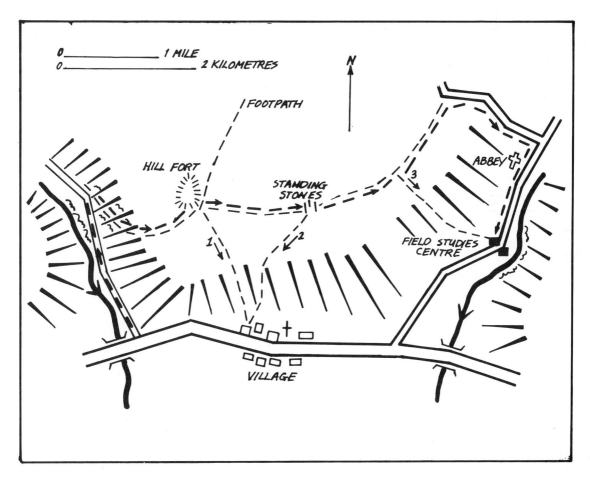

Figure 4.2 *A well thought out day's walking with a number of 'escape routes' built in*

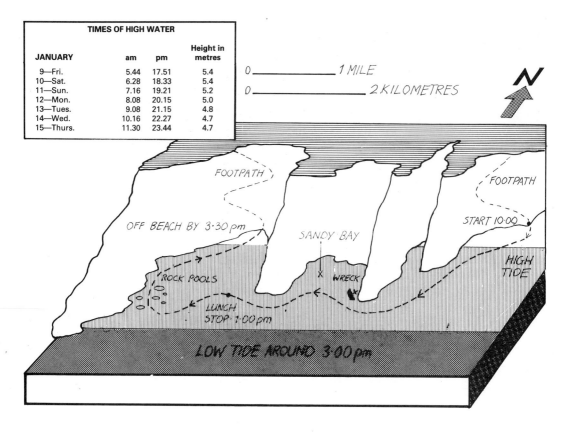

TIMES OF HIGH WATER			
JANUARY	am	pm	Height in metres
9—Fri.	5.44	17.51	5.4
10—Sat.	6.28	18.33	5.4
11—Sun.	7.16	19.21	5.2
12—Mon.	8.08	20.15	5.0
13—Tues.	9.08	21.15	4.8
14—Wed.	10.16	22.27	4.7
15—Thurs.	11.30	23.44	4.7

Figure 4.3 *Walking by the sea has its own hazards, particular care must be taken with the tides*

checked against local knowledge. Tide-tables are generally published in the local press for the current week, but for advance planning it is necessary to buy one of the separate booklets which give tidal details for the area for the whole year.

The general principle is that a walk should begin just after high tide and follow the tide out, thus ensuring that by low water you should be in front of a clear exit from the beach, with no risk of being cut off by the advancing waters.

Figure 4.3 shows a walk planned for Tuesday, 13 January. It begins just an hour after high tide and follows the receding waters at a respectful distance around the coast. Sandy Bay does represent something of a danger spot as it is on a part of the coast that is bounded by high cliffs with no paths up to the top. No matter how fascinating the

wreck might appear, it would not be advisable to linger here – the rock pools with their secure line of retreat afford a much safer place for leisurely examination. If the same walk were attempted at 10.00 a.m. on the Friday it would be a close run thing, and if a 12.00 noon start were made the party would almost certainy be trapped at 'X'.

Nowhere is local expertise more important than when dealing with the ebb and flow of the tide. The tide-table is at best an approximate guide and will give some indication of what is possible, however, in practice many factors can affect the rate of tidal flow up and down the coast. Anything more than a casual walk up and down the promenade needs to be checked out with the coastguard or harbour master's office in advance. Tides, of course, are not the only dangers on unplanned coastal walks: taking

Figure 4.4 *Beaches are wonderful places to explore so long as safety is well provided for*

advice may prevent you stumbling onto patches of unstable ground, trying to wade across unfordably deep inlets or even blundering into the remnants of a minefield from the last war!

Accommodation

When it comes to selecting the type of accommodation for your school trip a number of constraints have to be observed: the two most important of these are the cost and the location. In the case of a limited budget certain facilities will be outside your price range. If you are particularly interested in a certain location there may only be one kind of accommodation available, although one of the approaches I would like to suggest, that of 'creating' your own accommodation, can often step around both of these difficulties. Other more specific factors that may govern your choice are looked at in the

next section on preliminary visits. The venues examined here are ranked according to increasing levels of commitment demanded from the teacher organising the group.

Field study centres and hostels run by LEAs

An ideal starting point for those who are new to the business of field weeks is to patronise one of the centres maintained by their own education authority; most run two or three which cater for a variety of outdoor pursuits. They are generally very well organised with permanent full-time staff, most of whom are qualified teachers who can share the burden of 'round the clock' supervision. Particular emphasis is paid to the safety side of being out and about and they are often well equipped with a variety of resources. There was a time when virtually all such establishments were heavily subsidised and so offered extremely good value for money but, unfortunately, more and more of them are now expected to break even and some of the financial advantages have been lost. A further drawback is that it is often impossible to guarantee a week at the time of year of your choice unless you book a long way in advance, in some cases over two years! Some authorities insist on allocating times so you may find yourself having to make plans to travel at a time of the year that does not fit in with your overall planning.

Field study centres and hostels which are commercially run

There has been something of a boom in recent years in centres opening up to offer tailor-made field study courses to schools. Advertising material for these kinds of establishment comes flooding in through schools' letter boxes, especially in the autumn term. Before looking at what they have to offer, honourable mention must first be made of the Youth Hostels Association.

The YHA has been an introduction to our countryside for many young people. In the past it has had a somewhat austere and spartan image that was largely well deserved. Things have changed over the past few years as they have begun to cater for school groups completing environmental study courses. Not all hostels are set up to accommodate school parties who wish to use these kinds of facilities, but some 180 of the 260 hostels in England and Wales are suitable for practical work and 28 are designated 'Field Study Hostels' and have additional educational facilities. They can represent very good value, prices are reasonable, provision of resources can be good and the supervisory staff often have detailed local knowledge which can prove invaluable both during the planning stage and when on the ground. Normally one of the members of staff needs to join the YHA in order to book their group in. Full details of what is currently available can be obtained from the Education Department, Youth Hostels Association, Trevelyan House, St Albans, Hertfordshire AL1 2DY. Other charitable groups such as churches or conservation-based organisations do run hostels, but unless you are a part of the group it is difficult to get to hear about them.

If I sound rather cautious in discussing other privately run centres it is because some of them do need treating with great care. Most are run and maintained to high standards of comfort and safety with well-qualified and sympathetic staff, but some are not. What can you expect from a company who offer access to their residential environmental studies centre? Clearly there is much variation but a typical package would include: coach travel there and back and perhaps to selected venues whist there; accommodation frequently in chalets or caravans near the sea, perhaps in dormitories in converted outbuildings elsewhere; all meals including packed lunches where necessary; recreational facilities ranging from the extravagant to the rudimentary; and educational support sometimes of a rather patchy nature. Few establishments would operate without at least claiming to have all this on offer, but sadly on-site examinations can reveal, as is sometimes the case with holiday brochures, that all is not quite what it seemed.

Drawbacks can include: unsuitable locations – a site next to a busy main road or in the middle of a holiday camp waste land; poor standards of accommodation and cleanliness; large numbers of children from several schools putting a strain on what facilities there are; unpalatable food; questionable staff; inadequate educational resources and, above all, a sense of being institutionalised that would be hard to beat outside of prison! As in most things you tend to get what you pay for and the best centres can be very good and very expensive. However, if you come from a comparatively affluent area and perhaps plan a major trip away only once every few years, they are well worth considering. An establishment which charges well below the average could be offering a real bargain, but you would have to go and see the place first to be sure. Some companies offer activity holidays for children where they can choose from a variety of mainly sports-based options, but these have comparatively little to offer those wishing to undertake some kind of study of an area.

Hotels

Some hotels have moved into the 'school visits' trade after a series of miserable summers and a general migration of the British tourist abroad. Sometimes they are marketed by specialist companies who put hotels and schools in touch with each other and provide various forms of back up, sometimes they are just in business for themselves. They can be both very pleasant to stay in and fairly cheap. What we are looking at here is the kind of small family run seaside hotel, often in an old building perhaps on the sea front. The facilities will not be wonderful, the residents' lounge will become your class and common room, there will probably be little outdoor recreational space attached to the hotel and finding somewhere to park the coach will be a nightmare, yet there are many advantages. Your group will be self-contained, having taken over the whole hotel, and once the doors are shut for the night you know where everyone is. There is a kind of 'graciousness' about living in even a cheapish hotel which the children always seem to respond to and, in my experience, the standard of catering tends to be good, as are washing and toilet facilities. The real bonus of using hotels is that if you want to go to the seaside and are prepared to go out of season you can sometimes negotiate your own terms on a one-off basis which can prove very competitive compared to other forms of accommodation.

Indoor camping

Indoor camping is a concept we developed after several years of using established centres and hotels. The problem we had was that with regular field weeks, occurring at least once a year, the financial demands we were placing on parents were becoming excessive. Also, there were places which we had identified as desirable destinations, but where no suitable accommodation could be found. Our answer was to circulate churches, parish councils, schools and sports and social clubs in a given area with a view to hiring a hall for a week. The basic minimum requirement was sufficient floor space to sleep everyone, some kind of toilet and washing facilities on the premises and a kitchen. Chairs and trestle tables would be an advantage too. On our first outing on this basis we took over a church hall in a small town in North Wales and paid then £200 for the privilege. This was a welcome boost to church funds for relatively little effort on their part, and it enabled us to take the children away for under half the 'normal' price to an area of our choosing.

Of course there were many additional complications: we had to take all our own bedding and mats to sleep on; we had to erect temporary partitions from corrugated card to ensure privacy for the different groups; and we recruited two catering students from the local technical college to cook and serve our meals – food for which we had purchased in advance and taken with us. We shared much of the administrative burden of planning all this with the children and incorporated it into the learning experience. In doing this we established a model which has been successfully built on, on a number of subsequent occasions as an alternative to other high cost options.

Outdoor camping

Outdoor camping is a wonderful activity to pursue with children and there are many books which deal with the 'how to' aspects of this. If camping is to be done properly, with due regard to the safety and comfort of the children, them much of the week is necessarily taken up with activities directly related to the running of the camp. Now this may well be no bad thing, but it will cut down the time available for study. If you have to hire the bulk of your equipment, the whole business could work out almost as expensive as a week in a hostel – only tolerable if it is the experience of camping you are going for. Perhaps the best option for those who are mainly interested in the local study aspects is to get the best of both worlds by going for one of those establishments which offer pre-erected tents and other on-site facilities.

Making a preliminary visit

A preparatory visit to an area, whether it has been chosen for a day trip or a field week, is an essential part of the whole process of planning. Details of any accommodation need to be checked at first hand, outdoor activities need to be looked at on the ground and resource materials have to be collected that are unavailable elsewhere. The very fact that such a visit has been made, together perhaps with a well-presented slide show, can do a lot to set at ease those parents who may be concerned about their children going away, especially if it is to be a residential trip.

Such an initial visit should not be made too far in advance of the week itself, a severe winter can destroy whole sections of footpath at critical points in a planned walk, whilst summer fires may devastate whole areas of woodland or moor set aside for study. The normal progression of the seasons can change an area quite dramatically so that the pleasant woodland path of early spring is overgrown and impassable by late summer. The easy streamside walk in the frosty chill of winter or the baking heat of summer turns into a tedious quagmire following spring or autumn rains. Institutions and the people who run them also change so don't expect facilities offered one year to necessarily be available the next. If accommodation has been chosen, a preliminary inspection must

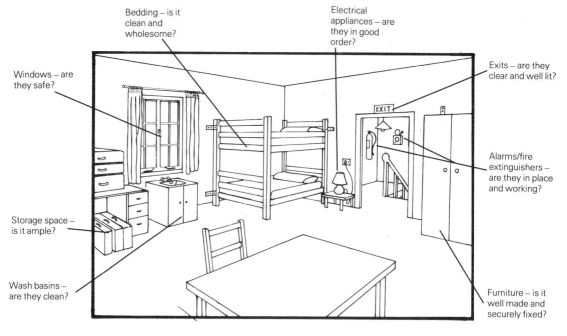

Figure 4.5 *There are lots of points to be aware of when inspecting accommodation*

be made to test its suitability. If a deposit has been requested try and withhold it until your visit, otherwise it may prove difficult to cancel your booking, should it become necessary, without financial penalty. Apart from the obvious things like general cleanliness, the most important factor to assess is the attitude of the people who are in overall control of the place and who will have most day-to-day contact with the children. Do they show a genuine interest in what the children are coming to do? Try to ask about the activities of other parties who have stayed. Do they remember them fondly or are they critical of the children's behaviour? Discuss the possibility of your group returning unexpectedly, half-way through the day, soaked to the skin and caked with mud. How do they react to the prospect of getting the children washed, dried and fed at short notice? Ask about rules, be wary of those places which have too many rules and those which have too few, neither will work terribly well.

Enquiries of a more practical nature mean actually counting to see if the washing and toilet facilities are adequate for the number you are bringing and rely on your own judgment rather than management assurances. I would not normally be happy for more than five or six children to share a single wash basin, or more than ten or twelve to share a single toilet. If baths or showers are to hand, spend a little time thinking about questions of organisation and supervision for whatever facilities are available. If there is enough hot water, washing can be done in shifts so make sure that supplies are effectively unlimited. Providing this last condition is fulfilled and that the children have brought suitable clothing and bedding, then central heating is not essential unless a visit in the depths of winter is contemplated.

If possible, try to beg a meal while you are there, as this will tell you something of the generosity of your hosts and the standard of their catering. In any event, ask for a specimen weekly menu and discuss what provision they can make for those on special diets. Many centres expect children to do a variety of domestic tasks such as setting tables, washing up and keeping their rooms and other areas clean and tidy. If this is the case ensure that the demands made on the group's time are not excessive and that if there are jobs to be done than the right 'tools' are supplied to do them with.

Discover what provision is made for the children's recreation. Is there a common-room for their use and an outdoor play area? We remove televisions wherever we find them and lock them away for the duration of our stay, others regard them as essential for the continuing sanity of the party! Look carefully into the bedrooms to see that they are 'wholesome', light, dry and airy. Obtain or make for yourself a plan and list the number of beds in each room so that you can allocate rooms in advance – careful planning here can save a lot of sleepless nights. Find out what bedding the hostel supplies and what the children are expected to bring, remembering that not all children have easy access to a sleeping bag. Whilst up in the bedrooms or dormitories ask about fire precautions and evacuating the building should it become necessary. Make sure that fire exits are unblocked and examine the fire extinguishers to see when they were last serviced. Some of the privately run residential centres sadly neglect safety measures of these kinds.

Finally, attention should be paid to the comforts of the hardest workers on any field week – the staff. Make sure that there is some kind of separate staff room into which staff can escape and which is equipped with the necessary items for making reviving cups of tea and coffee. Some centres, especially those run by LEAs, have their own staff who are able to supervise children in the evenings, for example, and give the visiting staff a break, otherwise the responsibility lies wholly with the qualified teachers in the party.

Decide whether or not everything advertised in the literature is actually there and working. If a fully-stocked laboratory or lecture room has been offered to you, it should consist of more than a hut with a magnifying glass or a blackboard and piece of chalk in it. If things do not seem right, then *now* is the time to ask. Be exacting in your inspection but also be realistic. Do not expect the hostel you have chosen on the side of a lonely Welsh mountain to have all the comforts of a five star hotel, expect no more than is adequate for your purposes. On the other hand, do not be fobbed off with excuses about facilities that are advertised but 'temporarily unavailable', you will almost certainly still be paying for them.

Although you must be prepared to use the preliminary visit to probe any weaknesses in the accommodation you have booked, it is also important to be aware of a place's advantages. The building itself may be of special architectural or historical interest, the immediate surroundings might be outstandingly attractive or members of the resident staff may have skills or interests they can share with the children. In practice, most centres catering for outdoor studies are well run and offer good value for money. Careful checking beforehand will do much to put out of business the few who exploit inexperience and our natural desire not to make a fuss in order to make a fast profit.

As time is bound to be limited during the first visit, unless of course you build your family holiday around it and spend a whole week there, certain priorities need to be identified. Any accommodation must come first. Certainly any museums, castles, churches or other places of interest on the programme ought to be visited, even if it is to do no more than peer through the door and engage the curator or custodian in conversation. This is also an opportunity to buy guidebooks and postcards and to negotiate special rates of admission for your party. Naturally a good look around is necessary if a thorough assessment of the place's educational potential is to be made.

Time spent in a local bookshop should provide a further crop of guides, maps and pamphlets on matters of local interest. A postal subscription to the local newspaper is useful, not only for getting the feel of the place but also for gaining advance notice of any custom, festival or special event that may be on during the course of the study week.

Our coach once overtook the splendidly barbaric Minehead Hobby Horse on its annual May Day foray, but by the time we had explained what was happening to the children it had turned down a suburban side street and vanished. A local primary school may be interested in forging some sort of link involving, perhaps, some initial exchange of letters between the children and then a meeting of some kind, educational and/or social during the week. The staff there will almost certainly have an invaluable store of local knowledge that they may be prepared to put at your disposal.

Further advice from a whole range of individuals can be sought either by post, by telephone or, best of all, by face-to-face meetings. These include officials working for the various rescue services: the police, coastguard, mountain rescue and so on; representatives of local societies which are involved with some particular aspect of the area; natural history, local history, archaeology; members of other amenity groups, ramblers for example; and people from the business community who may have an interest in your undertaking.

By the end of your preliminary visit you should have inspected and approved any accommodation, for which a deposit may now be paid, spoken to a variety of people and received all sorts of hints and tips, collected an armful of literature of different kinds and be carrying in your head some fairly detailed knowledge about the area you will be operating in. Above all you should return with a sense of enthusiasm for the place that you can communicate to the children, and which will keep you going through the weeks of preparation that still lie ahead.

If you are planning a residential visit you will now be in a position to finalise the programme for the time away. Studying the relevant maps before the trip should enable the organisers to set out an initial itinerary, which can be modified and other details added in the light of first-hand knowledge. Some intended activities may be struck off whilst new opportunities thrown up by the preliminary visit may be capitalised on. When it comes to assigning particular activities to particular days, you should be aware of the need to balance up the week. For example, if the trip up has been a lengthy one then the first day out should not be particularly strenuous, perhaps a little 'sight-seeing' to set the scene. If possible, days when the children are likely to get wet or muddy should be alternated with days of more sedate activities. The process is set out fully in the case study at the end of the book.

Preparatory work in the classroom

There are two main schools of thought about preparing children for extended visits. One takes the view that the more children know about the sites they are going to study, the more productive their investigations will be. The other maintains that the less they know about the sites, the more genuine their sense of exploration and discovery and the more meaningful their investigations. Staff must decide for each trip which emphasis they wish to give. If the children have examined plans and photographs of a castle they are going to visit, they will greet the site with a thrill of recognition, be able to find their way around and feel quickly at home and ready to begin their programme of work. An equally valid approach is for the children to arrive at a site knowing little more than its name, to be given a brief, and to be left to discover whatever they can about its construction and history. The groups will hurry off and each corner turned will bring a new discovery. My only personal observation is that I do believe that it is possible to over-prepare so that if the children have spent the last seven or eight weeks on it they begin to feel a little jaded about the whole project.

However, some preparatory work is essential in teaching the techniques of observation and recording, and in explaining as fully as possible details of how their excursion is to be organised. I feel that time spent away is precious and must be used as productively as

possible – half-way up a Welsh mountainside is not the best place to begin teaching children the correct way to use a 30 m tape-measure. Naturally, most of the skills exercised by the children while away will be part of their normal curriculum. However, there may be some special technique which you want to employ, taking bearings with a compass or surveying by triangulation, for example, which should be practised in the comfort of the school grounds.

The children need to be given as much information as possible about the layout and routine of the centre at which they are staying. This will do much to quell any early worries and will also remove the excuse, 'But I didn't know . . .' from anyone who does choose to misbehave whilst away. Once the team of adults has been put together, they should be introduced to the groups of children for whom they will be responsible, and the groups given a chance to work together both in the school and on a day's outing which can become, as suggested earlier, something of a dress rehearsal. In this way if there are problems of compatibility within any group then changes can be made to its composition before the week begins.

Packing – what to take

The lists overleaf relate to items which you might expect to take if you were spending a week away from home with a class of, say, thirty children. Obviously, on a day trip many of the domestic items are left behind, but even so, it is necessary to give the children guidelines as to what they should wear and also to think carefully about the range of educational equipment you will need.

Children's clothing

It is said that experienced travellers always travel light, however, the fewer the items taken, the more careful the selection of those items has to be. Advice needs to be given to parents as to what they should pack. Over the years we have evolved a fairly standard list which we duplicate and hand out with the suggestion that parents annotate it and stick it inside the lid of their child's suitcase.

Underwear	– enough for 6 days
Socks/tights	– 7 pairs
Indoor shoes/slippers	– 1 pair
Strong outdoor shoes	– 1 pair
Wellingtons (sometimes optional)	– 1 pair
Shirts/blouses for outdoor wear	– 5
Trousers/jeans for outdoor wear	– 2
Pullovers for outdoor wear	– 2
Waterproof top	– 1
Hat or cap	– 1
Scarf and gloves (if cold)	– 1
Set of clothing for indoor wear e.g. dress/ shirt and trousers	– 2 sets
Set of nightclothes	– 2 sets
Dressing gown (optional)	– 1
Soft toy (optional)	– 1
Handkerchiefs	– 4
Wash-bag including soap, flannel, toothbrush and toothpaste	– 1
A small back-pack	– 1
Plastic rubbish sack to pack dirty washing	– 1

Items which may be needed according to the type of accommodation planned include:

Hand towel	– 1
Bath towel	– 1
Swimming costume	– 1
Sheets	– 2
Pillow case	– 1
or alternatively:	
Sleeping bag with sheet liner	– 1

These lists were drawn up prior to a week away for which we had planned considerable outdoor activity in late spring when the weather could be distinctly changeable. As a break from damp and dirty clothes we suggest that parents pack some smarter items for indoor evening wear only, the concept of dressing for dinner may seem a bit outdated but it does wonders for morale after a wet day on the moors! For a similar week in July we might reduce the number of individual garments destined for outdoor wear and substitute shorts for one of the pairs of outdoor trousers and tee-shirts for some of the outdoor shirts and blouses.

We try to discuss with parents what are and are not suitable clothes and fabrics for what we have in mind. We tend to recommend trousers for both boys and girls when out exploring, and usually we have to put up with a large number of pairs of jeans, although denim is not a particularly good fabric for outdoor wear as it becomes cold and heavy and clinging when wet. Cords on the other hand are ideal. We also explain that it is better to have a number of layers of clothing that can be taken off and put on in response to changing conditions rather than one heavy coat which is on or off, and suggest a light-weight plastic waterproof top, which also offers some protection to wind, be obtained. Hats are useful, either to keep the head warm and dry in wet weather or to offer protection from the sun when it is hot.

It is easy for parents to get the idea that they have to rush out and buy a host of camping and mountaineering equipment for their children. There is of course nothing wrong in buying special clothing provided it is going to be used regularly. We do, however, caution against buying new boots or shoes for walking as the children will inevitably have a miserable time trying to break them in. We have, by the way, found that a sound pair of wellingtons, fitting snugly with good quality thick woollen socks, can be good for many miles of walking providing the terrain is not too uneven and rocky in which case the extra support to the ankles given by boots becomes important. We encourage families to swop items of clothing around to make good any deficiencies.

Fewer families seem to own suitcases now that plastic hold-alls of various types have become more popular. However, in practice a suitcase is the best container for the job – its rigidity helps keep the children's clothes reasonably neat and keeps any breakable items, such as souvenirs, intact. They are also easier to pack into the boot of a coach, can be sat on in an emergency and offer somewhere to stick the all important list of contents referred to earlier.

Each child may need some kind of bag for carrying around essentials such as clipboards, paper, pencils and packed lunches, and the best policy is to encourage families to buy suitable light-weight nylon back-packs for everyday use and then press them into service for trips away.

Should the child be taking any regular medication we always insist that it is delivered into our care with full written instructions as to its administration. Children who are receiving antibiotics or other treatments for acute illnesses should stay at home.

It is also important that you make clear what should not be brought. Some kind of rule against packing extra foodstuffs into cases should be considered as should a ban on radios and electronic games that make irritating noises. Personal stereos are a slightly different matter, as are cameras. The general principle with items of this sort is that it is clearly understood that the child is responsible for them and that they are sent along at the parents' risk.

Educational equipment

The sorts of things you, as teacher, are likely to want to take to support your exploratory work will, of course, vary depending on the kinds of activities you have in mind. Equally as there is always an element of genuine exploration it is as well to be prepared for the unexpected. Again we have evolved a basic equipment list which is supplemented when

necessary with additional items. This all packs into an old large tin trunk! The basic equipment needed for a class of thirty juniors on a week's study visit include:

Recording Materials:

Clipboards	– 30
A1 drawing boards (optional)	– 6
A4 paper/notebooks for notetaking	– 250 sheets/class set
A4 paper for sketching	– 250 sheets
A1 kitchen paper, various uses	– 100 sheets
A2 1 cm graph paper	– 50 sheets
Sugar paper for art work – various sizes and colours	– 100 sheets
Pencils (HB)	– 50
Packs of assorted coloured pencils	– 6
Sketching pencils (2B/charcoal)	– 10
Small tins of oil pastels	– 6
Pack of large coloured felt-tip markers	– 2
Waterproof marking pens	– 2

At the top of this part of the list comes a class set of clipboards. I consider some form of sturdy 'platform' on which the children can rest to take notes and sketch an essential item. Too often, bewildered children in wet and windy weather pace around behind their teacher giving their attention to trying to control flapping sheets of sodden paper and ignoring their surroundings. The simplest form of clipboard can be made in school by putting together suitably sized pieces of hardboard and bulldog clips. They are better than nothing but the clips do go astray. We have always invested in commercially-produced boards with a large sturdy clip securely riveted to the top. On occasions when we have expected wet weather, we have generally taped sheets of thin perspex to one side of the board which can be hinged to one side to allow working, but folded down in wet weather to offer some protection, whilst at the same time enabling the child to see the map or fact sheet they have in front of them. We have sometimes taken larger drawing boards if we see the possibility of more extended art or survey work being undertaken not too far from base. You may also want to consider the advantages of tying each pencil to a clip board, if you do you are far more likely to return with the thirty pencils you set out with.

Measuring equipment

Tape measures, 1 m	–	10
Tape measures, 10 m	–	2
Tape measure, 30 m	–	1
Trundle wheels (optional)		
Rulers, 30 cm for indoor use	–	10
Rulers, 1 m (optional)	–	6
Ball of string, nylon coloured (optional)	–	1
Magnetic compass, Da Silva	–	6

Clinometer, homemade or commercial	–	2
Small spring balance, to weigh up to 5 kg	–	2

Observing and collecting equipment

Small hand-held magnifying glass	–	15
Assorted self-sealing freezer bags	–	100
Assorted sealable plastic containers	–	20
Pooter (optional)	–	6
Hand nets (optional)	–	15
Plastic buckets (optional)	–	6

Special equipment

Cameras, still, cine and video
Tape recorders
Binoculars
Microscopes
Computers

You may choose to take along some more

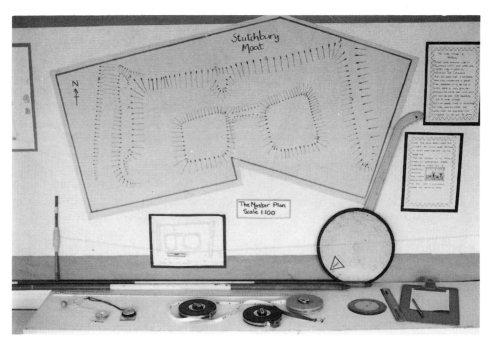

Figure 4.6 *Some of the different kinds of measuring equipment that are available*

Figure 4.7 *A variety of items to help with collecting can be taken*

elaborate pieces of equipment to help with the process of observing and recording. Most teachers will carry a camera as a matter of course. The children at work can be recorded on a series of slides which can form part of a presentation to parents and other children. Photographs can be taken to supplement the children's own drawings, in particular, as an aid to colouring when these are reworked back in school. Carefully positioned pictures can also help with activities such as model making whilst the odd atmospheric shot could act as a spur to memory for some creative writing. Some teachers have used the instant image facility of Polaroid cameras as an aid to on-the-spot observation and to help follow-up work in the evenings at the base. Better still, are those moments captured on cine or video camera, provided of course that you have easy access to one and are prepared for the extra weight and responsibility of carrying one around.

We have often reaped great benefits from having a small portable tape-recorder on hand both for recording the spoken words of a guide to some historical site, and for recording background sounds such as waves breaking on the sea shore or the wind whistling across the open moors. You may want to carry binoculars with you to aid your personal observations but be prepared for a lot of competition from the children who will want to 'share' it with you.

If you have secure accommodation back at base you may want to keep one or two microscopes there. The binocular type are by far the best for the kind of work likely to be done in primary schools. The inclusion of a computer is not as perverse as it sounds. I have heard of several teachers who have packed their computer and taken it away to use its data base facilities for compiling some kind of record of survey work undertaken. Obviously an important factor here is ensuring the security of valuable pieces of equipment and sensible precautions need to be taken by way of locking things away when they are not in use and marking them. Most people are familiar with the idea of security marking with inks that only show up under ultra-violet light, but a more practical way to deter any would-be thief is to plaster the name of your school all over the equipment in paint, perhaps together with a few tasteful flowers or the odd frog or two. This makes the item virtually unsaleable and so not worth the attention of most crooks.

Other supplies

Every school party planning to operate away from school needs to equip itself with a first aid kit. Quite often local authorities recommend or even supply kits for this purpose, otherwise a visit to one of the larger chemists will provide a wide choice. You will do well to have such a kit permanently on standby for school journeys which will then free you from the vagaries of whatever your destination has to offer. If you envisage breaking your party into a number of small groups, operating semi-independently, then it is worth making sure that every adult has a small pouch of basic supplies so they don't need to refer to you for every minor cut and graze. You may also need a lockable medicine chest should you have responsibility for administering any drugs; the children's medical cards, filled in by their parents, can also be kept in here. Depending on the age of the children you may wish to pack some sanitary towels, as it is not uncommon for the stress of being away from home to bring on some of the older girls' first periods and you should be prepared for this eventuality.

Contents of small first aid pack:

   Sterile adhesive dressings in a variety of sizes
   Non-adhesive sterile absorbent dressings
   Bandages: ordinary, triangular and crepe
   Cotton wool
   Roll of sticking plaster
   Scissors
   Tweezers
   Safety pins
   Cream or spray for treating insect bites.
   A plastic bottle of distilled water may be carried for washing minor injuries if you are likely to be away from sources of clean water.

Room should be made for an assortment of other items as your mountain of packing begins to totter. A few torches are useful for keeping an eye on things at night without switching on all the lights – in case of an emergency they could prove invaluable. Another piece of safety equipment which should be issued to each adult is a whistle. This can be used for communication between groups and individuals according to a pre-arranged code and can also be used to give the recognised distress signal, six blasts on a whistle, repeated once a minute.

A couple of boxes of books, some for recreation and some for reference should be included. A selection of board or card games for indoor relaxation and some basic sports equipment, a couple of large balls perhaps, for outdoor play ought to be taken. Of course, if you have opted for an indoor type camping trip then your list of requirements will be so long and will vary so much according to individual plans that there is not the room to consider it here. The drawing up of such a list will be so closely tied in with the planning process that the two will go hand in hand.

5   Management on the Trip

The journey

Although there are alternatives, outlined earlier, I am going to discuss the ins and outs of travelling by coach, as this is the most common choice.

A successful and trouble free coach trip begins several weeks before the children actually set foot on the vehicle. The first step is to make early contact with the company who are taking you and to explain your requirements. If you know of a driver who has given you good service in the past, ask for him or her by name. Getting a sympathetic and understanding driver is half the battle, someone who will drive steadily without crawling, who will stop as and when called on and who always has the comfort and safety of

the children in his or her mind can make the difference between a disastrous outing and a pleasure trip.

The next step is to agree the route with the driver well in advance, you may have driven it yourself and looked out for suitable stopping places. On a journey of several hours we generally like to make three stops, assuming an eight o'clock morning start. The first stop is a brief one for toileting about ninety minutes to two hours into the ride, say, between ten and eleven o'clock. A generous lunch break of up to an hour which allows time to picnic, use the toilets and have some playtime would be planned for probably around one o'clock. We always try, where possible, to fit in a stop at some scenic spot or historic monument mid-way through the

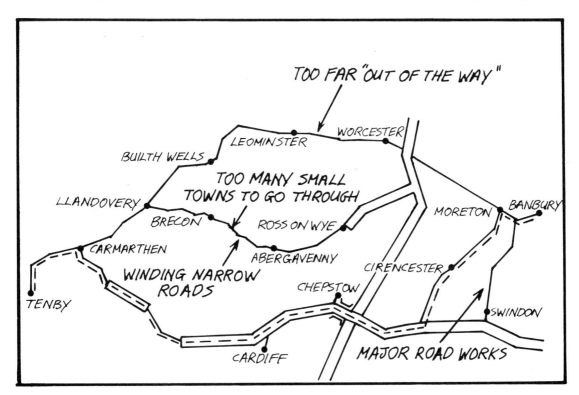

Figure 5.1 *The route for the journey there and back needs careful consideration*

afternoon, again to break the journey and also to provide a focus for interest when the tedium of travelling is really starting to tell. We would be aiming to arrive in time to unload, do some unpacking and enjoy our first evening meal away, say, between four and five o'clock.

If you are a member of one of the major motoring organisations, it is well worth enlisting their help in the planning of the route. Not only can they advise you of the best route to take, but they can also give you information about hold-ups due to road-works which may not be apparent from the maps you are studying.

Once you have established a route and a programme, go over it with the children. You can even give them a printed timetable with a number of counting and 'I-Spy' type activities to help the journey pass by. Such a sheet can also form the basis for a mathematical study of the journey in terms of miles covered, average speed, petrol con-sumption and so on. You will need to make it clear that work with the sheet is optional as some children will become ill as a result of reading during the journey.

Complete your packing a day or two before so that on the morning all you will need to put into the boot are a number of sealed and labelled boxes. Advise parents of the importance of making sure their children get a good night's rest; whether they eat a hearty breakfast or not is up to them, parents should know what suits their child best before a long journey. Most children benefit from taking one of the proprietary anti-travel sickness pills and for some it is essential. Don't forget to ask parents to give you supplies of similar pills for the return journey.

On the morning of departure, and indeed throughout the trip, it is important to try and maintain a calm and settled atmosphere. The causes of travel sickness are not fully understood but there is little doubt that undue excitement is often a contributory factor. We normally try to leave fairly early, before the rest of the school arrives and forms a send-off committee. If you were anticipating an eight o'clock departure, ask for the coach to arrive at least half an hour early to enable you to get your equipment loaded and to have any last minute consultations with the driver. The children and their families should arrive between five and fifteen minutes before departure, give their cases to the driver to be stored in the boot and take their seats ready to wave goodbye at eight o'clock when the coach hopefully pulls away. On occasion, with particularly helpful coach companies, we have arranged to load all the luggage the night before so that all the children need to bring in the morning is themselves and their hand luggage. Few things get a trip off to a worse start than having to stand around waiting for a coach that is late. If the coach fails to arrive, institute enquiries immediately as to the nature of the delay and consider asking the parents to say their farewells and get the children to sit down and wait in their classroom.

You will need to specify quite carefully what is to be packed in their hand luggage. Normally, there will be a packed lunch, something to drink, some other assorted snacks and perhaps a comic or book to read or some simple games which can be played on their laps. A good deal of common sense has to be exhibited both by the children and their parents over the choice of refreshments.

Once the last waves have been waved and the school fades into the background you can settle down to a trouble free journey. However, it is as well to bear in mind that even with the best of preparations, on the day, it could all be too much for some children and they could be ill. The problem with travel sickness is that it is contagious, and unless the situation is handled efficiently one child being ill could set off several others by chain reaction. It is a good plan to keep the front two seats clear and let the children know that anyone feeling unwell should tell you at once so they can be moved to the front of the coach. This change of scene with a clear view ahead frequently causes the symptoms to subside. In case it does not, you should be prepared with two large plastic buckets with sawdust at the bottom, a cardboard box or plastic bag containing extra sawdust, two rolls of paper towels, a box of large tissues, a bottle of drinking water and a small bottle of disinfectant. Should anyone actually be ill you should, by deft manipulation of these items keep the problem under control.

A calm and settled atmosphere during the trip helps to keep sickness at bay and for that reason alone rowdy behaviour should be severely discouraged. However, to keep on top of developments adults need to be seated throughout the coach rather than clustered together at the front. The key position is the middle of the back seat from where practically everything can be seen. For the same reason we generally ask the children not to sing on long trips, not only does it act as a distraction to the driver, but it can also exacerbate several raging headaches that will have come on during the course of a long journey. From a safety point of view, children must not stand up in their places, kneel on their seats to face backwards or walk about the coach unnecessarily.

Accommodation – settling in

On arrival everyone is likely to be bursting with excitement and perhaps other needs. First, however, the teacher in charge needs to establish contact with the management, inform them of their arrival and discover if there are any last minute changes to the arrangements agreed on during the preliminary visit and subsequent correspondence. As probably the only member of the party with experience of the site it is important to make yourself generally available during the early stages of settling in to iron out any difficulties as they arise. The children should know who they are sharing rooms, huts or caravans with and should be escorted from the coach to their sleeping quarters to unpack. Point out the toilet facilities on the way. The children will be getting used to their new surroundings and it is helpful if the other adults can postpone their own unpacking in order to

offer a reassuring presence to them. We make an arrangement to ring someone on duty at school with the news of our safe arrival so that concerned parents can ring there for news. There should be some kind of common-room where all the children can assemble to meet any centre staff and be reminded of any rules relevant to the establishment, particularly those dealing with safety.

The first evening away is an important time, and what happens during it and the period leading up to bedtime can set the tone, for good or ill, of the entire week. We have found it best to make the evening quite full, leaving the children little time to worry too much about feeling homesick and to tire them out so that they will find no difficulty in falling asleep in strange surroundings. Providing the weather is friendly we often use the first evening to take a walk around the immediate vicinity of the centre. If the weather is not so good we may spend a little time talking about the area, but will then push back the furniture or find a vacant hall and play some fairly energetic games, finishing with something that slows the pace right down before preparing for bed.

When talking to teachers it is clear that one of the most stressful periods for them is bedtime and getting the children settled down and asleep. There is no need to put up with children rampaging around at two in the morning provided a little planning is undertaken. First, always make clear well in advance the correct timetable for going to bed. It has been our normal practice to get ready for bed by gathering all the children together at a quarter to nine for a hot bedtime drink and a biscuit. As they finish they are gradually sent in twos and threes to wash and change into their nightclothes with staff generally being around to supervise. Everyone is on their way by nine o'clock.

At a quarter past nine the lights are put out and story time begins. For many years now we have ensured peaceful nights by spending half an hour or more reading stories to the children by torch light. Obviously, if all the children are in a single large dormitory or in smaller rooms opening off a central landing only one member of staff will need to be involved. If sleeping arrangements are more complex other story tellers will need to be drafted in. The selection of suitable stories for bedtime reading is quite a crucial one, as is the tone of voice used. Above all it is necessary, especially on the first night, to be patient and keep on reading. Once you feel that the majority of the children are asleep you can stop reading out loud and announce in a soft voice that you are going to sit quietly and carry on reading your book until everyone is asleep and that is exactly what you do. On rare occasions you may find that a particular child resists all attempts to go to sleep, in which case you might suggest that the child would be better sleeping on his or her own somewhere so as not to disturb the others.

Once the children are all settled, normally about half past ten on the first evening but as early as half past nine towards the end of the week, there is an opportunity for the staff to relax together, perhaps share a drink, review the happenings of the day and go over the next day's programme. It is vital for the well-being of the staff that they have this all too brief measure of free time. Periodically someone will need to check the sleeping children to ensure that all is well. I always prefer to have staff sleeping accommodation closely integrated with the children's so that if there are any problems in the night the children know where to find a friendly adult.

Accommodation – establishing a routine

On the first morning many of the children will wake up very early, there is not a lot that can be done about this, and it tends not to happen later in the week. We normally place a ban on anyone getting up before seven o'clock and try to make sure that everyone has a few comics or a book by their bedside to occupy them should they wake before 'getting up' time. For a few days you and your colleagues really are totally 'in loco parentis' and you must therefore be prepared to take on the duties of a parent and ensure that the children wash at suitable intervals and change their clothing regularly.

We always try to ensure that the children wash before breakfast and put on their outdoor clothes, and that at the end of a day out the children wash again and change into their indoor clothes. If the weather has been particularly chilly or the children have become unusually muddy, we try to get the children showered or bathed before supper. The way you go about this rather depends on the facilities to hand. Showers are more efficient both in terms of time and use of hot water, and baths may have to be rationed. You should also be aware of the additional safety hazard presented by wet and slippery floors at bath times. If we are roughing it and only have the option of wash basins, we try to fit in an evening coach trip to the nearest swimming pool so that everyone gets thoroughly clean all over at least once during the week.

Enquiries amongst the parents should have revealed the presence of any potential bed-wetters. Covers to protect the mattress should have been installed and spare bedclothes ready to hand. The problem is not uncommon with children away from home and should it occur you will need to be reasonably discreet about checking the state of the bed and if necessary stripping it, remaking it and organising the washing of the soiled bed linen. We have felt a little awkward on a number of occasions about greeting parents on our return with armfuls of clean bedding and the explanation that their child was fine whilst away and the extras were not needed.

At some time before or during breakfast somebody will have to obtain the latest weather forecast, either from the radio or by ringing the local weather centre. On the basis of the forecast and on direct personal observations you will need to make a final decision on which plan you are going to put into force for the day. After breakfast you may want to hold a briefing session for the whole party to go through the day's programme and to pick up on any general management points that have occurred to the staff. After that, it is on to the bus or out through the front door, having remembered, of course, to tell somebody where you are going.

Having returned to your centre after a busy and successful day, what next? Nobody is pleased to see the return of a party which streams in shedding muddy clothes and boots in all directions. When you arrive, a routine for removing and drying damp and dirty clothes must come into play. An area should be set aside as a drying room, there may even be a purpose made one if your centre is well run. Damp tops should be hung up together with muddy trousers and socks, and indoor shoes exchanged for dirty boots. As there is an element of undressing here you may choose to send boys and girls in separately, in any event numbers should be controlled to avoid a scrimmage developing.

After the first day's outing we like to set aside some of the evening for work and some for recreation. A typical timetable might begin with the main meal of the day being served at six o'clock. By a quarter to seven it is all over and a group will probably be helping with clearing the tables and washing up. The others return to the notes and sketches they have made during the day and will spend some time amplifying their records by writing additional notes, completing pictures, drawing up maps and plans, identifying shells or leaves, looking up information about the birds they saw and reading about some of the places they have visited in guidebooks or other works of reference. At eight o'clock we will call a halt to all this, although some find it difficult to stop, and finish off the day with some games, a walk, a quiz or some music and singing. By now the children have done everything once and are well on the way to becoming old hands and settling in for the rest of the week.

One concern that is frequently expressed by parents and children is that they will become homesick while away and that this will spoil the week for them. In practice we have found that with careful planning and sensitive management the problem hardly ever arises. By keeping the days full and the evenings busy we try to avoid too much time for brooding. The general air of excitement and the positive support that exists within the groups also helps. We usually ask parents to write to their children while they are away although we prohibit the use of the phone in all but the most exceptional cases. We write home and to the school during the first or second day of the trip to share our news with them and also try to make some time towards the end of the week for the children to shop for small presents for their families.

Group organisation on the ground

One of the biggest challenges that a teacher can face is moving large numbers of children safely around the town or countryside on foot. If they can make the experience educational as well as safe they should really feel a great sense of satisfaction. My basic recipe for achieving this is to ensure that the party is accompanied by sufficient adults to give a ratio of one adult to every six children. Although I might consider walking down the road with thirty children and two adults, one in the front and one at the back. I certainly would not go far and I certainly would not expect to get anything done. Our normal practice is to divide the children into five groups of six. The teacher who is in charge of the excursion moves off with six children followed a short distance behind by the first of three groups under the control of another adult, two more groups follow on and the rear is brought up by the second teacher or other responsible adult. The spacing between the groups will vary depending on conditions, but it is advisable that all of the adults in the party are in sight of each other most of the time. What follows may seem over-regimented, mathematical even, but with a little thought and practice it becomes a natural and

Figure 5.2 *Each group can be organised differently according to where they are walking and what activities have been planned*

perfectly practical way to move about.

Let us assume for the moment that the coach has pulled up in a lay-by. There is a fairly busy main road to cross and a stile to climb, and the party has to follow a rather indistinct footpath across three fields to a small nature reserve. This has to be crossed, paying particular attention to the trees growing there, in order to reach and explore the ruins of a nineteenth-century saw-mill. Afterwards there is a steep walk down through some woods to reach a small town

where the coach is picking us up.

The children have been told in advance whose group they are in, (they may even have it written down), and get off the coach in those groups to gather with the adult concerned, as far away from the roadside as possible. After the coach has pulled away the teacher in charge, who has done the walk before, leads off along a wide, well-metalled footpath by the side of the road. The children walk as three pairs with the accompanying adult behind them, each group is separated by a distance of about three metres. When the time comes to cross the road the groups cross separately, each adult being responsible for seeing their children safely over the road (or bridge, stile, stream or whatever the barrier may be). Obviously the other adults who are waiting will lend a hand keeping an eye open for traffic. There is a stile to climb over to escape from the roadside. If there is some potential hazard, such as knee-deep nettles or inquisitive cattle, the adult with each group should go over first but should remain by the stile to offer support to the children should they need it as they climb over. It is important that the group in front is not crowded, so the other groups maintain a discreet distance until it is their turn to surmount the obstacle.

The fields prove to be free of any potential danger and offer firm easy walking along the line of a poorly defined public footpath. The children can now walk in a much looser formation remaining, however, with their adult and apart from the others. As the country is open the groups may well spread out to ten metres apart or more. The experienced teacher stays in the lead because the route would not be clear to someone who has not been over the ground before. Because the path through the nature reserve is a narrow one each group now moves in single file and the gap between them closes.

On arrival at the site of the ruined saw-mill the groups gather together for a general discussion, they then explore the remains as a group, working as a team on the various tasks set. The adult acts as advisor and assistant to the children and is the main arbiter of where the group can and cannot go. After a period of exploration and recording the groups set off again. This time, as the path is well marked and there is no chance of a wrong turning, the group leader brings up the rear and is therefore in a position to ensure that everyone is off the site and continuing down to the pick-up point in town.

This may all sound very complicated but the principles are clear:

- Each adult is responsible for his or her own group which stays together.
- The qualified staff responsible for the whole party position themselves where they can remain in control and 'do most good'.
- The groups adjust the distance between themselves and the actual formation in which they are walking or working to suit conditions.

In the course of a day-trip, or even an entire week, the groups will tend to stay the same. Obviously this means that considerable thought has to be given to the composition of the group, but once they are established they can begin to learn to work together as a team.

Other points about moving safely and productively across country are covered elsewhere, but there are certain things about group management which cannot be stressed often enough:

- Make your plans well in advance based on first-hand experience and stick to them.
- Your plans should be sufficiently comprehensive to allow for some flexibility should conditions change.
- Make your plans as widely known as possible and ensure that there is a responsible individual back at base who knows where you are going and who can take action should your party fail to return. Remember to tell them when you do get in.
- As the leader of the group you should be continually monitoring the condition of your party and following the relevant plan.

This is a system that really works and has been tried and tested on many occasions. Other ways have been attempted and abandoned for one reason or another and we have had encounters with other school groups which have been exhibiting all the symptoms of total breakdown of control – some of them were lucky to return home with as many children as they first set out with. Some school parties have not been so lucky.

6 Activities on the Trip

It is not my intention here to give a lengthy account of those methods of work that are bread and butter to teachers, rather I want to concentrate on some of the practical tasks that relate closely to field study work but may be less familiar.

The scientific response – Measuring and surveying

From an early age children become familiar with a whole range of methods of measuring but sometimes these need to be applied in particular ways should they wish to determine the height of a tower or draw a plan of a pond.

Children are often introduced to measuring by using different parts of their bodies to record sizes, and then the method is dropped in favour of the superior accuracy of the standardised metric system. This is a shame because the ability to use your own body to measure is extremely useful in the field, bypassing the need to carry around additional equipment, and actually producing surprisingly accurate results. The most useful measurements are the inch, the span and the pace. Of the three the pace is subject to greatest variation for any given individual because of the natural mechanics of walking and the different surfaces and gradients encountered. Even so, on reasonably even ground and with a little practice, good results can still be obtained.

Figure 6.1 *Different parts of the body can be used to make useful measurements*

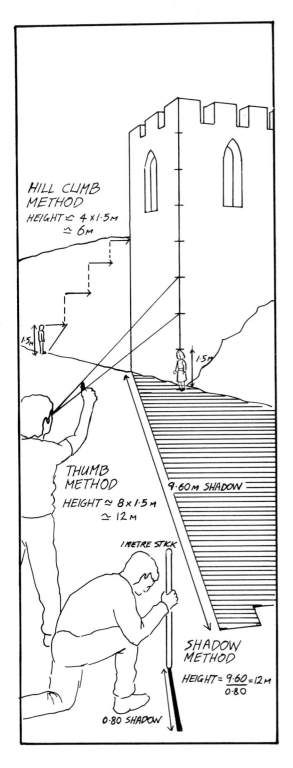

HILL CLIMB
METHOD
HEIGHT ≃ 4 × 1·5M
≃ 6M

1·5M

1·5M

THUMB
METHOD
HEIGHT ≃ 8 × 1·5M
≃ 12M

9·60M SHADOW

1 METRE STICK

SHADOW
METHOD
HEIGHT = $\frac{9.60}{0.80}$ = 12M

0·80 SHADOW

Figure 6.2 *There are a number of easy ways to find heights*

Of course, a whole plan could be drawn up purely in terms of 'personal' measurements but it probably becomes more useful if it can be redrawn in standard terms. To do this a correction factor has to be applied, the average size of a pace can be determined by using a tape to measure 100 paces, then dividing the measurement by 100. Normally a calculator will then be needed to convert the paced out measurements into metric figures.

$$100 \text{ paces} = 62 \text{ metres}$$
$$\therefore 1 \text{ pace} = 0.62 \text{ metres}$$
$$\therefore 28 \text{ paces} = 28 \times 0.62 \text{ metres}$$
$$= 17.36 \text{ metres}$$

Similar calculations can be used to find the size of an average inch or an average span but remember these figures only apply to a particular individual at a particular time.

Questions about the height of buildings, trees or cliffs often arise and there are a number of roundabout ways to arrive at an answer, apart, of course, from climbing to the top with a tape measure between your teeth. Children should become accustomed to estimating measurements and can be quite accurate if there is a scale of some kind for comparison and they are far enough away to be able to make some adjustment for the change in angle as their eye approaches the top. Supposing one of their class mates stands at the bottom of a tall tree and they back away until the size of the child matches the height of their thumb at the end of an outstretched arm. They can then use that thumb as a measuring rod to express the height of the tree as a multiple of their friend's height.

If the object in question is something that can be walked up, like the side of a hill or the ramparts of a hillfort, then they can use their own body height as a reference point. This involves the children standing at the bottom and staring at a point which is, as near as they can judge, straight ahead. Fixing their eyes on some small landmark such as a tuft of grass or a twig they then walk to the spot and repeat the exercise. This continues until they reach the top when they should have a rough idea of the height expressed as a multiple of their own height.

If the weather is sunny a quick calculation can be made by comparing the length of the shadow of an object of known height. The calculation for a church tower would work like this:

$$\frac{\text{length of tower's shadow}}{\text{length of known object's shadow}} \times \frac{\text{height of}}{\text{known object}} = \frac{\text{height of}}{\text{tower}}$$

$$\frac{6.40\,\text{m}}{1.60\,\text{m}} \times 1.90\,\text{m} = 7.60\,\text{m}$$

Equally the answer can be found by doing a scale drawing (see Figure 6.2).

If an accurate answer is needed and the sun is not going to cooperate, then a clinometer is called for. This is a piece of apparatus for sighting along, onto which is fastened a plumb bob and a scale so that the number of degrees away from the horizontal can be read off. They can either be purchased or made in school.

The person using the device squints up at the top of the object whose height they wish to find along the sight. A friend may then be needed to read the degree of tilt. Before the height can be found a further measurement needs to be made: the distance from the observer to the base of the object. The actual height can be calculated with trigonometry but most people find the height by means of another scale drawing (see Figure 6.3).

Having a map or plan of a site, be it a ruined castle or a meadow full of flowers, gives the children a powerful tool for asking and answering a whole variety of questions. If they have had a hand in making that plan they will have become thoroughly acquainted with the site and be in an even stronger position to understand it. There are a number of survey methods of differing levels of accuracy and complexity that children can learn and apply, working as part of a team to quite ambitious projects. Here are some general principles which apply to all types of map making:

- Walk around the site first and produce a sketch plan. In many cases this will be as

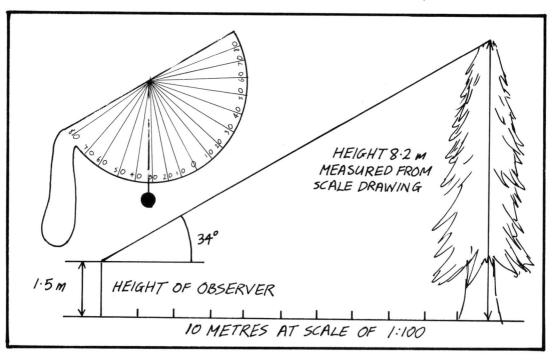

HEIGHT 8·2 M MEASURED FROM SCALE DRAWING

34°

1·5 m   HEIGHT OF OBSERVER

10 METRES AT SCALE OF 1:100

Figure 6.3 *With the help of a clinometer heights can be determined from a scale drawing*

far as the children will need to go, a bird's eye view may be quite an imaginative effort for young children but with experience they will get used to some of the conventions of plan drawing and the use of abstract signs to convey information. By pacing out certain crucial dimensions they will begin to appreciate some of the more formal techniques of plan making.

- Always work from the whole to the part, in other words, plot in the outer boundaries of any site before starting work on the detail, the same principle incidentally holds good for sketching.
- Whenever possible have independent checks on vital measurements.
- Always record on any notes you make, as well as on the final plan, the name of the site, the date, the names of the surveyors, the direction of north and the scale.
- Work slowly and systematically!

These principles apply to the three main methods of plan drawing which can be used with children of primary school age:

Planning by offsets

The outline of a standing building, scattered remains of a ruin or the positions of trees in a park could all be plotted using this method. Measurements are taken at right angles to the base line along which is stretched a second tape.

Triangulation

This is a method which also uses a baseline, but this time once it is set up a long tape is fastened to each end and the location of

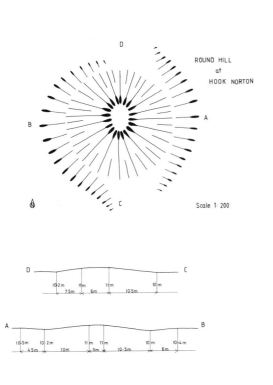

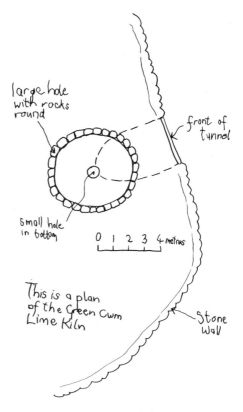

Figure 6.4 *Plan drawing can be done at a number of different levels of ability*

Figure 6.5 *Children at work making a plan of a medieval village site*

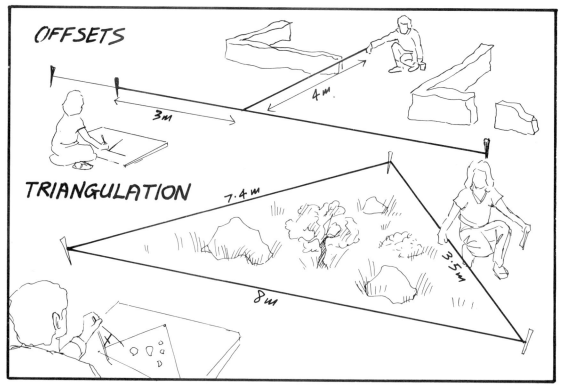

OFFSETS

3m

4m

TRIANGULATION

7.4 m

3.5m

8m

Figure 6.6 *Different survey methods*

particular features recorded with a measurement from each tape. The plan is drawn on site by reducing the measurements to scale and drawing them as arcs with a compass, the position of the object is fixed where the two arcs intersect.

The planning grid

If there is a large amount of fine detail to be plotted, for example the children may want to record the distribution of wild flowers within a certain area or perhaps plan the fractured remains of an old pavement, then you could consider marking a grid out on the ground. This can be done in a variety of ways, either with a square frame on to which the lines have already been tied or with nails and string or even with chalk. Once the grid is in place the children may draw what they see under it directly on to squared paper.

So far we have looked at measurement purely in terms of distance and area. There are of course many other 'properties' of the environment which can be subjected to measurement.

Most children will already have had considerable experience working with thermometers but they can extend this in various ways: studies can be done to show how temperature changes from place to place and from time to time; looking at questions about altitude and wind strength and direction, a graph could be drawn of temperature against the number of people lying on a given area of beach; the course of a stream could be looked at with accurate measurements of water temperature along its length.

A hygrometer is a device for measuring relative humidity, that is the amount of water vapour in the air expressed as a percentage of the amount of water there would be if the air was saturated. The simplest hygrometers consist of a circular dial with a pointer from which the percentage humidity can be read directly. They are not as accurate as the more elaborate 'wet and dry bulb' models but are

far more robust and easier to use. They can be used in general studies of the atmosphere and weather or to look at particular locations, to compare the growing conditions in a narrow rocky ravine with those on the exposed hillside close by for example.

There are further devices which are used primarily in relation to investigations of the weather. A barometer records atmospheric pressure, a measure of the weight of air pressing down upon it. The children will be able to see its use as a tool for the forecasting of changes in the weather, this is particularly easy on the coast or from a vantage point high in the mountains where they will be able to see the weather coming from a considerable distance. A barometer can also be used as an altimeter and the children might like to examine ways in which pressure changes with height on a trip perhaps from sea level on to the hills.

An anenometer measures wind speed and there are some quite expensive professional models with three rotating cups mounted on a handle above a scale which may give readings in miles per hour or metres per second or as points on the Beaufort Scale. Home-made versions can be made on a rotating pattern in which case fairly accurate readings can be made at slow wind speeds by counting the number of rotations and calculating the result like this:

$$\text{Wind speed in metres/second} = \frac{2\pi r \times R}{T}$$

Where: r is the length of the rotating arm as a decimal of a metre.
R is the number of rotations counted.
T is the time in seconds for which the rotations were counted.

Unfortunately with high wind speeds the number of rotations gets increasingly difficult to count, the children may like to apply their technological skills to solving this problem. An alternative pattern can be made which will give relative measurements in terms of the displacement of a board, pivoted at the top and hanging vertically.

A trip to your local garden centre will

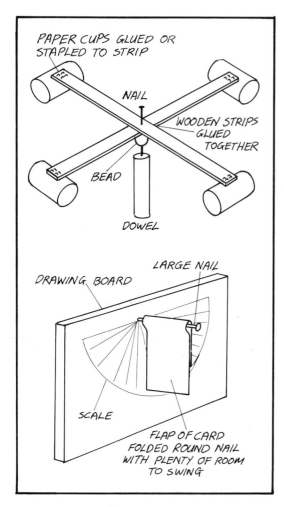

PAPER CUPS GLUED OR STAPLED TO STRIP

NAIL

WOODEN STRIPS GLUED TOGETHER

BEAD

DOWEL

LARGE NAIL

DRAWING BOARD

SCALE

FLAP OF CARD FOLDED ROUND NAIL WITH PLENTY OF ROOM TO SWING

Figure 6.7 *Home-made anenometers*

Counting and questioning

Many queries that the children will have can be answered by simply counting – how many arrow slits in the castle wall or how many mushrooms growing in a ring. Some counting tasks may become impossible because of the large quantities involved, for example, the number of sea shells on the beach or the number of dandelions growing in a meadow. In these cases the children could be introduced to the idea of counting within a sample area of between one and one hundred square metres and then, by working out the whole area of the beach or field, calculating a total figure:

Number of dandelions in sample
square metre = 18
Area of field $\simeq 65 \times 32$ square metres
$\simeq 2080$ square metres
$\therefore$ Approximate no. of
dandelions $= 2080 \times 18$
$= 37\,440$

Calculations of this sort will lead the children to consider questions about how typical their sample area is and whether they need to count several squares and take an average, as well as the concept of answers which are approximately right; in the example above it might be appropriate to quote the answer as 'about 40 000'. It is always worth encouraging the children to make estimates or 'thinking guesses' in cases like this, initially for the practice in grasping large quantities and later as a check on the likelihood of their answer being near to correct.

Questions sometimes arise about percentage cover – clouds in the sky or lichens on gravestones. The second example is important in pollution studies where the degree of lichen cover reduces as the air gets dirtier. The usual way to assess this kind of thing is visually by comparison with a standard chart showing different densities of cover.

Some quantities have to be determined over a period of time – the number of birds feeding at a table, the number of cars passing along a stretch of road. Here the children will

enable you, for a few pounds, to buy a couple of very useful little tools for studying soil conditions. One of these is a pH meter which will tell you the degree to which the soil is acid or basic. This is a useful measure when comparing the flora of other regions and when trying to account for differences. The other tool is designed to tell you if your potted plants need watering but it can be used to compare the amount of moisture in different soils. If the children become especially involved in studying factors affecting plant growth then a photographic light meter will help them to compare the amount of light that different patches of ground receive.

need to have a way of maintaining a continuous count. One of the oldest methods is to make a tally; if they are working on paper vertical strokes can be tied together on every fifth count by a diagonal slash which makes the final reckoning that much more speedy. You can use mechanical counting aids whereby clicking a lever advances the number displayed by one. Some people have used calculators in a similar way setting them up to repeatedly add one when a key is pressed; this is fine providing the other buttons can be avoided. One of the hardest parts of this kind of record making is keeping the children's interest engaged, and this can be done by giving them partners to work with and having changing shifts, perhaps every ten or fifteen minutes. In these circumstances the children will expend a lot of ingenuity to design automatic counting devices.

The business of counting becomes even more involved under conditions where the nature of the item counted is important and not just its presence. Suppose, for example, you are interested in the species of bird or the make of car, then it is probably worthwhile doing a little preparation and putting together a pro forma on which results can be entered. Such a document can be helpful in giving the child some idea as to what to look out for and it could involve brief 'definitions' or some pictorial references.

Some of the most subtle pieces of counting that children can be asked to do relates to the collection of data about people through the medium of a questionnaire. Again, these demand a lot of work in advance to determine the scope of the questioning and a lot of tact in the administering of them. The party may be interested in where people have travelled from to visit a tourist spot or they may want to enquire about the range of work done by people they meet in the market square of a country town. The questions should be kept brief and to the point and asked with unfailing politeness. It is never a good idea, however, to allow young children to approach strangers in this way unless they are under the direct supervision of an adult. We have used our basic groups in this way with the

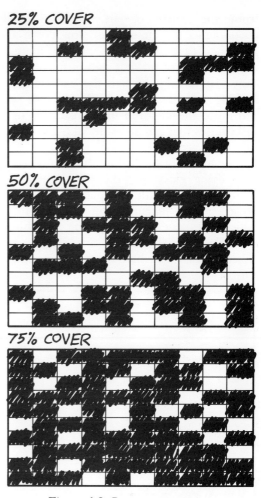

Figure 6.8 *Percentage cover chart*

children operating in three pairs within two or three metres of the supervising adult.

Observing and collecting

One of the key skills that we expect our children to develop is that of being able to make effective observations – so many people 'look without seeing'. The experience of taking on a new environment is one through which the children can be encouraged to really begin to look closely at their surroundings. There are a number of techniques to help them with this, many of them drawn from the world of art. By continually encouraging the children to slow down and take their time over a task you will increase their chances of making significant observations. By talking through the experience of looking closely at something you can introduce the children to the excitement of discoveries that can be made 'in front of their noses'.

The most obvious aid to observation is the magnifying glass, but the way in which it mainly helps is a little unexpected. Most hand lenses offer a magnification of times three, which does not reveal anything invisible to the naked eye although it may clarify some 'fuzzy' areas. Its chief contribution lays in focusing the observer's attention on one particular spot by surrounding it with a frame. We have found little difference in the quality of detail of drawings of small leaves done through magnifying glasses as compared to those done with the aid of cardboard frames! A view can be temporarily framed by the fingers but as a general aid to observation we take a piece of cardboard about 20 cm × 15 cm and cut out a circular hole 4 cm in diameter at one and and a rectangular hole 6 cm × 4 cm at the other. The round hole tends to be used for close observation of tiny objects while the rectangular one is peered through to help with distant views of buildings or landscapes.

Figure 6.9 *Children using an observation frame to concentrate on a view*

When not in use the frames are kept on the children's clipboards.

Of course, telescopes, binoculars and microscopes really do transform a viewpoint by giving significantly enhanced views, but the importance of the frame is still relevant. The problem with these aids is that there are rarely enough to go round although you may be able to supplement your stock with examples brought in from home. Also, do not forget that a camera viewfinder can be used as an aid to observation, particularly if it is in a single lens reflex camera with a magnifying lens attached. Sometimes it helps to get to grips with a scene by looking at it from a different angle, upside down by looking through a magnifying glass held at arms length or, an old artists trick, reversed in a mirror. Observation games can be played at times which might otherwise prove rather unproductive, during the coach journey perhaps using the idea of a certain number of points for roadside features noted.

We should perhaps be encouraging children to make all their observations in the field, teaching them to interfere as little as possible with the object of their observations. There is, however, a natural urge to collect and providing this is carried out under certain conditions it can become a valuable part of learning. It is important, though, that everyone in the party is clear about what cannot be collected.

Rocks and fossils are popular objects to collect, but care must be taken first during the act of collecting, as pulling one rock loose can have a catastrophic effect on the others piled up above it, and secondly one should be aware that there are certain sites which have designated sites of Special Scientific Interest (SSI) from which you should not remove specimens. The beach has always been a happy hunting ground for collectors of shells, pebbles and driftwood, but do caution the children, some nasty things get washed up on beaches these days.

Legislation prohibits the uprooting or destruction of all wild plants except on the part of authorised persons, normally the landowner. This means that while you can weed your own garden, you may not pull up the same plant growing elsewhere. In addition, there are some sixty or so plants listed in the Wildlife and Countryside Act 1981 from which flowers or leaves may not be picked. As some of these rare plants can appear, to the untrained eye, similar to more common species, or because people may be familiar with them as cultivated varieties, mistakes can be made. As a general rule you may choose not to allow the children to collect wild flowers, even of the commonest type – after all, thirty children descending on a bluebell wood can make quite a hole in the display of blossoms. We do sometimes collect single specimens of common flowers which have been securely identified for later study but this is very much an activity under close adult supervision. Plant materials which can be collected include fallen or dried leaves, fruits, nuts or seeds – in moderation – and fallen twigs or branches.

It is an offence to take or trap, injure or kill any wild bird, or damage or destroy its nest or eggs. Otters, red squirrels, and all species of bats are protected by the law against direct injury and interference with their breeding places and shelters. Other mammals have partial protection or are protected at certain times of the year. In addition, the smooth snake, sand lizard, the great crested newt and the natterjack toad enjoy full protection and it is against the law to interfere with other reptiles and amphibians on some occasions. This means that any school party needs to tread warily when exploring the natural landscape, not of course out of fear of any legal penalty, but out of a concern for our wildlife – all of which is under threat to some degree. The general principle is move carefully and quietly, otherwise you won't see anything anyway, keep your distance and do not interfere. In many ways children learn most about the wildlife of the countryside by acting as detectives and observing and reading natural signs. Children can collect hairs snagged on fences or gates, or feathers, partially eaten foodstuffs such as nuts and pine cones, footprints by preserving them in a plaster cast, and even in some cases

Figure 6.10 *One of the best ways to become acquainted with a natural environment is by pond dipping*

droppings, particularly owl pellets. Amongst the litter of the countryside you may also be lucky enough to find skeletal remains or shed reptile skins.

Some of the smaller inhabitants of the countryside remain 'fair game' for school groups, these have become generically known as 'minibeasts'. These are often collected for closer examination under a hand lens or microscope and may even be kept for a few days under suitable conditions to study their behaviour. If you decide to let the children collect in this way make sure that any habitats are returned to their undisturbed state: stones that have been turned over should be carefully lowered back into place and the piece of bark that has been levered from the rotten tree trunk is reinstated. When the children have finished their studies the creatures should be returned to wherever they came from. The larger 'minibeasts' such as slugs, snails, and beetles can be gently encouraged or rolled into a collecting bottle with the end of a finger or a pencil. Smaller

creatures can be sucked into custody with the aid of a pooter. Butterflies and moths should not be taken as children rarely have the delicacy of touch to avoid damaging them.

Pond dipping is a popular way to investigate the myriad of life forms that swarm through some of our waters in the summer months. The basic equipment consists of a variety of nets, some with long handles and some with short, white enamel or plastic trays for examining the catch and screw-top bottles for removing specimens for further viewing. Again the principle is one of causing minimal disruption to the environment. From the safety point alone, any work along the edge of ponds or lakes needs to be closely supervised. A number of methods are employed to catch different sorts of animals. Pulling a long handled net gently underneath the growing fronds of water weeds will bring in one group of animals, whilst digging deep into the muddy bottom will reveal a different fauna. Some creatures are too small to be picked up in a net and must be taken in samples of pond water. All organisms should be returned to their place of origin when they have been finished with. It was at one time common practice to collect frogs' spawn and keep it in the classroom to watch its development. In view of the alarming decrease in the numbers of the common frog this is no longer an acceptable activity.

In all of the work we do in the natural environment the accent should be on respect for the other living creatures we share our island with.

The creative response – Image making

People sometimes ask why, with cheap cameras widely available, should anyone go to the trouble of drawing anything? If we are going to go to the trouble of teaching children how to sketch we must have an answer ready, in fact there are two main answers relating to different functions of sketching. First, in making a sketch we are necessarily being selective, we are pulling out certain features from amongst the background detail and accentuating them, we can also at the same time interpret what we see and give a stronger form than it actually has in 'real life'. A person looking at a sketch of a landscape or a building prepared under these terms should come away understanding more of what they had seen than if they had simply viewed a photograph. The value of this kind of view can be enhanced by annotating the drawing with written comments. The second reason for making a sketch seems to be opposed to the first reason, for through the medium of a sketch we can, if we choose, rework reality not so as to reveal greater objective clarity, but as a way of saying something of our own emotional reaction to what we see. Children need to be aware of and encouraged to explore the different ways in which sketching can be used. The starting point is however the same. Often children who are considered to be good drawers, working neatly and precisely to copy or trace or repeat a favourite

design, prove to be poor at sketching. There is such a thing as being too confident at the beginning. The first attribute of a good sketcher relates back to an earlier section, they must be able to observe effectively. The first lessons in sketching can be done without pencil or paper at all, it is primarily a question of taking time to look and this is as true in the classroom as half way up a mountain.

Now the drawing can begin and, as in map making, the principle of working from the whole to the part holds good. The children can use their pencils to trace in the air the outline of the chief component of what they are about to sketch, they can than transfer that outline to the paper by 'tickling' it with the point of the pencil, beginning with a faint ghostly image which they gradually darken as they work their way over it. Now subsidiary details can be filled, faintly at first then more heavily as confidence in the accuracy of the line grows. Now it is time for the really fine detail, worked carefully in with the point of the pencil and finally any shading of textures and areas of dark and light that are necessary.

If the children have some specific purpose in mind for the sketch and you have been able to talk it through with them they can work it in on site. For example, suppose there is the facade of a ruined castle to draw, if they know that it is to be the starting point for an architectural model they will pay particular attention to getting the proportions exact and may well include some measurements and notes about building materials. If they are going to turn it into a back drop for a play about ghosts they will work on the shadows and perhaps accentuate the height of the towers to give them a menacing feel.

One of the constraints that children often have to work on during a field trip is shortness of time. This makes it even more important that they are well schooled in the art of looking first. It also means that once they have started they have to work quickly. You may have been fortunate enough to have set aside a whole afternoon for sketching but it is more probable that in order to capitalise on the experience you have a whole host of things in mind that must be accomplished.

The children may need to see their field sketch as a starting point which can be developed back in school. This means that once the thing is complete in outline with a few visual notes about shading they will have to be prepared to leave it.

One other form of instant image making which can be worthwhile is the taking of rubbings. Traditionally it is brasses on a church floor that are treated this way but many other surfaces can be covered in strong thin paper and rubbed with a thick soft coloured wax crayon: gravestones, manhole covers, brick walls, tree trunks and so on. These produce attractive images in their own right and useful references for when the children begin to recreate their experiences visually back in the classroom.

Figure 6.11 *Once back in the classroom rough sketches can be reworked to produce finished pieces*

Language

There are many different ways in which language can be used to respond to an event but overall there is a broad division which parallels that in image making, between the factual report or explanation on the one hand and the emotional response to it on the other. During the course of any particular trip you may expect children to use words in a variety of ways or you may prefer to concentrate on one particular kind of language. We have run weeks where the children were expected to keep a detailed and strictly factual diary-like account of their explorations, but have also been away when the children were asked to respond to what they saw with poems that would eventually be worked into their own personal anthology. We have always tried to avoid the trap though, that is so easy for teachers to fall into, of equating language with writing!

If a child has nothing to say, he or she will generally have nothing to write and we certainly cannot expect interesting and mature pieces of writing from children if they have never had a chance to hold our attention in conversation or discussion. Of course teachers feel uncomfortable because talk has an intangible quality, you cannot put it up on the wall at the end of term, yet it is essential. The various adults leading the groups have a heavy responsibility here, to monitor the conversation that is going on within the group, to join in with it and where necessary raise its level by asking questions, interjecting observations, making comments and generally keeping the pot boiling. Equally, they cannot afford to kill off the habit of listening by endlessly talking at the children rather than to them. A small portable tape-recorder can be endlessly useful for carrying around and recording children's first verbal responses to a place and any subsequent discussion that may develop.

In a more formal sense there may be occasions when the whole class has to participate in discussion and the children have to learn to wait their turn to make their point and then to do so briefly and tellingly before their peers lose interest. If you find that chaos tends to intrude into your class discussions you could adopt an idea used by the castaway boys in Golding's *Lord of the Flies* where some ceremonial item is selected, in their case a conch shell, and only the person holding the item at any particular time is allowed to speak. Sometimes it is useful to ask the children to give a short account to the group of some particularly significant discovery they have made or even to prepare a short talk on the subject to give to the rest of the party. Finally, the importance of the spoken word can be reinforced by inviting the children to read their written work back to each other. No matter what they come to write they must have a sense that each piece of writing is for a purpose, something that we will touch on in the next chapter on follow-up work.

If your expectation is that a part or the whole of a day or week will be reported on factually then you will have to give the children a structure within which to do that. They will need a notebook close at hand to jot down times, names of places and people and other relevant facts, and they will need the skills of a journalist to check on the truth of what they are writing, whilst at the same time editing out the uninteresting and trivial to give a robust and engaging account of their doings. Of course, all forms of writing shade into each other and their account would be excessively dull if there was no room for the odd phrase of description or a few lines reflecting on their personal feelings.

You may choose on some occasions to narrow down the range of responses the children can make in order to record some very specific pieces of information. When this sort of approach is called for a duplicated question sheet can be drawn up and given to children to fill in as they make the relevant discoveries. This is fine so far as it goes, but some school parties seem to use it continually to the exclusion of any other method of recording.

As well as reporting on the week as a narrative of their personal doings the children could also use broadly the same style

Figure 6.12 *Extract from a child's diary*

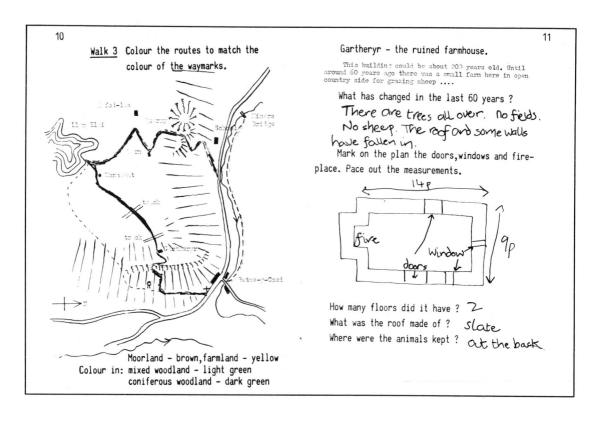

The handwritten worksheet content:

Page 10:

Walk 3 Colour the routes to match the colour of the waymarks.

Moorland – brown, farmland – yellow
Colour in: mixed woodland – light green
coniferous woodland – dark green

Page 11:

Gartheryr – the ruined farmhouse.

This building could be about 200 years old. Until around 60 years ago there was a small farm here in open country side for grazing sheep ....

What has changed in the last 60 years?
There are trees all over. no fields. No sheep. The roof and some walls have fallen in.

Mark on the plan the doors, windows and fire-place. Pace out the measurements.

14p

fire
Window
doors
9p

How many floors did it have? 2
What was the roof made of? Slate
Where were the animals kept? At the back

Figure 6.13 *An example of a completed work sheet*

to report on any discoveries that they make, perhaps on the history of a lighthouse or the habits of a deer in the forest. Here they will be drawing on the skills of the researcher who draws material together from a variety of printed sources and rewrites it in the light of their own understanding and experience.

Again, much the same factual style can be used to bring alive some incident which has kindled the imagination and can now be presented in narrative form to the reader as if they were there: the wreck of a fishing boat, the demolition of a proud monastery or the prowling of a hunter on the forest floor. A different sort of response can be called upon when the children are invited to use their descriptive powers upon a scene, again real or imaginary. Here it is not so much capturing the flow of events that matters, as being able to recreate a sense of being there, of a moment in time trapped in the text. A wide vocabulary and a flexible approach to its use is important in all forms of writing and

The Farm Buildings

The farmhouse was surrounded by all kinds of old ramshakl buildings. There were two Timber barns with huge wooden beams holding up tile roofs, some little brick pig-sties with slate roofs and a funny shed for carts with a thatched roof propped up on bundles of twigs. the yard was cobbled and spread over it was some straw. It was verey muddy in places though. The farmhouse stood in the middle of all this but looked clean and smart as if it didnt belong in this dirty old farmyard.

Figure 6.14 *A piece of descriptive writing arising out of a school visit to a farm museum*

will no doubt have been worked on in the past. Now, in the presence of so much that is new and exciting the teacher has an ideal opportunity to draw words out from members of the group, so that their shared vocabulary is enlarged, as well as injecting additional words of their own.

Finally, perhaps the hardest discipline to master – poetry. Most attempts to define poetry will fall by somebody's criteria but it must be something to do with registering an emotional response to a person, place or event through language which draws extra meaning from the pattern of sound it makes. The very fact that there is an emotional component makes it difficult to turn poems on and off like a tap. How many adults would respond gleefully to the command that they write a poem? Yet we expect it of children all the time. Most authors begin by imitating someone else's style so it is important from an early stage to read plenty of poetry to the children to give them a wide range of models on which to base their own efforts. We have tried in the past selecting suitable sets of poems to read while sitting on a stormy shore, under the shade of an ancient oak tree, by the side of a busy construction site or inside a ruined house getting towards midnight – you can do that sort of thing once you escape from the classroom!

Once they have been given a few clues about what poems are, the children can make a start. The task set should match both their interests and character and the circumstances they find themselves in. Everyone will probably have something to say about their teacher stepping back off a rock and into a mountain stream, but only certain children will want initially to write about the small flower growing in a rocky crevice or the blood-stained blade of some ancient knight's broadsword. Part of the function of teaching poetry is to extend the range of the children's responses so you should find that with plenty of good examples, including the work of their class mates, the children become increasingly open to new experiences.

Just as a sketch can be worked on to improve and finish it, and even reworked to produce new images, so can words be poured over, added to and edited until a polished product results. Children should always be encouraged to see a piece of writing as work in progress, something that can be returned to and rewritten, continually refining what they have to say and how they say it. This used to be a slow and painful process when each version had to be written out longhand. Now most children have access to word processors and should be familiar with the progression from first draft, which they may have jotted in a notebook sitting on the wall of a Roman fort in the Lake District, to the 'final' version which may be read in the classroom three weeks later.

Drama and music

Because we are used to seeing the performing arts displayed in purpose-built auditoria we tend to lose sight of the fact that drama, dance and music originally belonged under the open sky. Some staff may feel that drama begins and ends with the end-of-term play, but it can, in fact, be a powerful way of interpreting and responding to the environment. Drama sessions out and about can be as open-ended as you like. A way many people start, and there is quite an industry in this today, is dressing the part when they go to visit an historic site. It may be as medieval monks to tour a ruined abbey or as Edwardian farm workers to tour an agricultural museum. Having established a basic sense of empathy with these characters from long ago the next step is to inject a narrative element, perhaps by working to a prepared script, or by leading through certain situations by an actor or actors in period costumes.

Obviously the children can take part in far less ambitious dramas, some of which can almost be thrown together on the spur of the moment: storming the fort's gate, pulling drowning sailors from the cruel sea or mourning at the graveside of a young child who dies of cholera. The drama does not

The Bulldozer's Dream.

Why was I made a Bulldozer?
Why was I made a big yellow machine?
All I do is push the mud
It's not fair. Why couldn't I have
been made into something else?
I would have liked to be made
into a car.
Cars are lucky. They get to
see the sea the sea or even the
country. But all I see is mud
Now my days are over for here
I lie in the scrapyard
But maybe someone will come
and make me into a car.
That is my dream, to become a car
But i don't think my dream will
come true

Prehistorics.
Are all the prehistorics dead?
No, I saw one yesterday,
churning fields and shredding hay
Ironing down fields with its great wheels.
it turnd to come my way.
should i stay?

Thing
The giant thing rears up
it shovels up the earth
like a living dinosaurs.
it makes me feel very small.
like a midget.

I'm the mud!

I'm the Slurping burping mud.
I drip and I drop,
I Slip and I Slop
and I never Stop!,

I'm the creeping Steeping mud.
I flop and I flout
I plop and I pout
and you better Watch out

I'm the.....
oh no!
But the Sun comes out
and dries the mud up
Summer has come
my day is gone

Machine........

I don't like that useless
machine.
All it does is make patterns
in the earth.
It's noisy, dirty and it(s) Smokes.
It's a bit like a vicious dog Snarling.
growling at you.
I don't know what people see in
them.
TRAMPLE, TRAMPLE
CRUNCH, CRUNCH
Spoiling the grass
CHEW, CHEW.
Eating all those pretty flowers.
Well I hope they choke it!

Figure 6.15 *Example of children's poetry written whilst on a building site*

always need to be dramatic; by dressing in costume and acting out routine tasks, perhaps in mime, as they would have been carried out on the factory floor or in the castle kitchen can create a feel for the 'quiet' times in history as experienced by ordinary men and women.

Drama can also be used to open up imaginative horizons. Contemporary adventures can be set up blending treasure hunt with role play. Following the discovery of a coded message in a bottle we once acted our way to the top of a small Welsh mountain in pursuit of a mysterious dragon made of gold. My part was to keep the clues coming and pose various threats to the success of their enterprise by suggesting that the path ahead was blocked or the ruined cottage they had to pass was enchanted. An exercise like this can also be an excellent vehicle for problem solving in a technological sense as, for example, when they had to cross a small plank bridge without touching it with their feet!

There is a point at which drama shades into dance and here we are opening up to the children yet another way to respond to the environment they are exploring. The very movements of the children themselves struggling across a hillside in a strong wind become a kind of dance, but this can be refined and polished by an experienced teacher into a performance which can carry the feel of the great outdoors into the classroom or school hall. Ask children to move about their hall floor like falling autumn leaves, to the sound of a disembodied voice on the radio, and few will take the suggestion seriously. However put them in a wood as the leaves are falling around them and they cannot help but move naturally. It is partly a question of being aware of possible situations that may arise which the children can move with, and partly a question of setting things up, but naturally you never tell anyone else that you have been dancing!

We have sometimes taken musical instruments out into the wilds with us. Drums and recorders can help create the atmosphere of a medieval feast in the manor house hall whilst a familiar tune on a common-place instrument can sound quite unearthly when played in the heart of a densely packed pine wood. Sometimes we have taken our percussion instruments out with us, on a day that is guaranteed to be sunny of course, and have used them to improvise sounds to tone in with the rushing waters of a moorside stream.

As with other more scientific techniques all of these creative activities need to be prepared for, sometimes over a period of years, before they can come to fruition in a busy car park or on a lonely hillside somewhere. Nobody should expect drama work, for example, to be an instant success just because the children have landed up somewhere exciting. However, with the right kind of background the children can turn out performances that would put the National Theatre to shame.

The importance of doing nothing at all

There is a famous story which tells of the arrival of a new girl in class. She is being shown around by an 'old hand' when she takes a step towards the rabbit's cage she has seen in the corner. She is pulled back with a hissed warning, 'Don't go near the rabbit or you'll have to write about it!' There is a sense in which we as teachers ask for too much from our children. We instinctively panic at the sight of a child who doesn't actually seem to be doing anything, either because we believe in the old adage that the devil finds work for idle hands or perhaps because we have just seen what we are expected to cover next term under the national curriculum. I have attempted to show the wide range of activities that can be drawn in to enhance the learning experience out of the classroom, but children also need time to reflect and absorb and imagine, so please do try to give them the mental breathing room to make the most of their trip. Why not astonish them every now and then by replying to the chorus of 'Do we have to write about it?' with an 'Of course not!'

7   Following Up

For the most part any individual day trip or a full-scale field week becomes the main spring for a whole series of follow-up activities which keeps the class humming for anything from a week to the rest of the term. The trip itself is regarded as a chance to collect data and the follow-up involves processing that data and most importantly communicating the results to the wider community. There are other ways of looking at the value of the field week and of seeing it primarily as a social exercise, in recreational terms, or as a set of experiences to reflect on, in which case follow-up work will form a comparatively small part of the package.

By this time you should have decided, with the children, what form the final work is going to take. There are many options, each of which can be developed separately as a whole class exercise or, alternatively, you may feel it appropriate to let individual children adopt the method of presentation most suited to their interests. Usually we aim for each child to complete a sewn 'topic' book. This contains their writings and illustrations of aspects of their week away. It is then hand bound in a hardback cover. There are many other kinds of handmade books which may be more suitable for particular pieces of work, from the fan book to the concertina book. Occasionally loose-leaf files are used into which both the children's own work and other collected materials can be inserted. Sometimes we have worked towards putting all the information into a single printed booklet, much as a research team might collaborate on an academic paper. Occasionally the main thrust of the follow-up does not result in a 'publication' at all, instead an art exhibition or a concert or a play can be staged.

Rewriting rough notes, and sketches

One of the factors that will affect the quality and quantity of the work the children bring back with them from the field is the comparatively short time they will have had to collect information – the prehistoric stone circle that a professional team might have a week to survey is examined by the children in half a morning! This means that one of the first jobs upon your return is to look at their sometimes fragmentary notes and skeletal drawings and rework them while the memories are still fresh. There may have been opportunities to begin this process one evening while you were away, but if not, the children will need to get together in their groups and begin to compare notes.

Of course, if you are lucky enough to be able to hang on to some of the adults who came on the trip you are most fortunate, because they can then act as a chairperson to draw out the children's memories and help edit them into a coherent account. Otherwise the time will have to be structured to enable the children to do it themselves. Let us imagine that we have decided to adopt the diary approach to the basic record which is then amplified by further research.

It is Monday morning, the dinner monies have been collected in, assembly is over and you are ready to start. The children gather around tables in their groups. On the first day they were away they visited a lifeboat station and heard of a particular spectacular wreck and rescue which took place during the First World War, and in the afternoon they passed by the site of the rescue. They begin by reading the notes, probably slightly torn and sea-stained and, through discussion, remind each other of other aspects of the visit still in their memories but which were not written down at the time. Additional help is at hand because the teacher has written up an information sheet for that day which reminds them of the timing of events, the spelling of any proper names and any other points that have to be covered. Finally there is another chance to hear the gravelly voice of the elderly lifeboatman who showed them around, because the teacher took the precaution of taping his remarks. They may add some scribbled comments to their original notes or they may carry the additional information in their heads, but they are now in a position to attempt a first draft of their written coverage of that day.

This process of reviewing, sharing, collecting extra ideas and information can be used to improve any written notes, be they outlines for a story, a description of a steam engine or a poem about a motorway, either on a whole-class basis, in groups or even in pairs. The solitary worker can plod on alone but the quality of his or her work will probably suffer through lack of additional input from people who were there. Give the children a platform to communicate their ideas at an early stage and then open up to them the possibility of importing extra material before committing themselves to a written version.

The position with their embryonic sketches is slightly different; here additional support can come from other members of the class but of course they may not have shared that particular view-point so there are fewer possibilities for a fruitful exchange of information. Much of what they need to do can be accomplished alone. If there are several identical windows in their picture but they only managed detail on one, they can now fill in the rest; if they worked on a small corner of the roof to show the texture of the tiles, they can now extend it to cover the rest; and if they indicated that the end wall of the building needed heavy shading by scribbling across it, they can block in that shadow. If colour has been added in places, the pencils can be found and the colouring completed, and any annotations scribbled in the margins can be deciphered and rewritten so that they are clear.

You may well have to intervene yourself to help the children interpret elements of their drawings relying either on your own visual memory or on photographs. There are so many 'Instant Print' establishments ready to develop your photographs and have them back to you within the hour that you should be able to have them to hand from day one of the follow-up. Do be wary though about handing them out indiscriminately, or you may end up with thirty identical views influenced by the same picture. The same is true of postcards or pictures from reference books – they are there to be consulted, not slavishly copied.

In some instances the sketch may be so badly torn or stained with unpleasant looking substances that a totally new version is called for, in which case do not overlook the benefits of tracing or photocopying. In many cases these sketches will be works of art in their own right, but their primary function is to act as a source of visual reference for later work.

Processing data

You may have included in your programme a lot of work where statistical information of one kind or another was collected: you may have analysed the traffic flow through a busy town centre, recorded the gravestones in a country churchyard or counted seabirds along a stretch of coast. Now the children have to decide what it all means and present the information so that others can appreciate their findings.

Most teachers are perfectly at home with using graphs to represent visually and mathematically different kinds of information but it is not always easy to select exactly the right kind of graph for a particular purpose. A pictograph uses numbers of easily identifiable images to represent the count. Often the direct correlation is simply between the number of images and not their sizes. Bar charts represent information through columns or bars, the height or length of the column related to the quantity it is representing. A histogram shows the frequency of particular items and the quanitities are related to the area of the columns. When you have to represent amounts which vary against each other in a continuous way, such as temperature against time then a line graph can be used. However, if you were looking at average temperature as calculated for each month then a bar chart would be more appropriate. Pie charts are best employed when representing quanitities as parts of a whole as with percentages.

The answer to the problem of handling large amounts of data which relate to particular named individual items is to create a card index, probably arranged alphabetically. There is some justification for setting up a card index if the children have never done so before as it is a useful introduction to some of the principles of data handling and retrieval, but on subsequent occasions the children should begin to work with the school's computer and a database program. With an effective program not only can you ask the computer to sort, order and print out your data in a number of ways, but you can also ask it to select certain items of data according to quite complex sets of criteria: how many seed eating birds visited the birdtable on Tuesday when it rained?; looking at the gravestone record, what were the names of the men who lived to be over seventy and were born during the nineteenth century? Questions of this nature can be answered 'manually' but only after a tremendous amount of card shuffling. In fact, the better programs also come with graph drawing packages to so the whole process can be carried out from the keyboard should you wish.

Precise details of how to set up a database will vary from program to program but there are a number of common problems which should be examined. An important lesson to be learned about data processing is that although the computer can move the data about at high speed, it cannot normally go out and actually collect the information. This is the children's function and they have then

```
Bird Survey  -  Horley Reserve ( 20/5/87)

Note - Numbers refer to number of first
sightings within one hour period.

NAME      :Blackbird
SCI. NAME:Turdus merula
FLIGHT    :12
GROUND    :8
TREE      :3
FOOD      :Ground insects and worms

- - - - - - - - - - - - - - - - - - -

NAME      :Magpie
SCI. NAME:Pica pica
FLIGHT    :9
GROUND    :3
TREE      :12
FOOD      :None seen

- - - - - - - - - - - - - - - - - - -

NAME      :Kestrel
SCI. NAME:Falco tinnunculus
FLIGHT    :3
GROUND    :0
TREE      :0
FOOD      :None seen

- - - - - - - - - - - - - - - - - - -

NAME      :Blue Tit
SCI. NAME:Parus caeruleus
FLIGHT    :5
GROUND    :0
TREE      :7
FOOD      :Old seeds and buds

- - - - - - - - - - - - - - - - - - -

NAME      :Crow
SCI. NAME:Corvus corone
FLIGHT    :15
GROUND    :9
TREE      :3
FOOD      :Rubbish on ground

- - - - - - - - - - - - - - - - - - -
```

Figure 7.1 *Computer print out of information gathered on a trip to a local nature reserve*

got the job of telling the computer what they have discovered. The quality of the computer's 'answers' is a direct reflection of the quality of the children's information and the accuracy with which they have typed it in. On a big project the entering in of data can be extremely tedious! Normally some kind of shift system is necessary, perhaps a pair of children working together, so that they can check each other, for thirty minutes to an hour depending on their powers of concentration. If used for longer than an hour the number of mistakes begins to rise dramatically. It can be a difficult time when one shifts hands over to another, and you will probably need to be on hand to make sure that there are no misunderstandings about where the old group leaves off and the new one picks up. At the end of the day, because the computer record has to be accurate, you may find yourself having to review their entries in a final check for errors – and there will be plenty.

Image and model making

The first part of this next section is primarily a list of possible techniques you may like to use to recreate a variety of images arising from your visit. There is not the space here to give a detailed account of particular methods but some useful books are listed in the bibliography.

The initial sketches can be redrawn in a variety of media, with softer pencils, charcoal, coloured pencils, pen and ink or pastels. They may form the starting point for paintings in water colour or any of the other paint types available in the classroom. Other images may be transformed into collages with paper or fabric. You may want to select parts of certain images to print, either as lino prints or screen prints. Some elements may start the children off on pieces of sewing which could, in turn, incorporate tie-dying or batik. The same piece could be reinterpreted again and again in different media or else a high level of expertise could be built up by concentrating on just one approach.

Once back in school you will probably have a number of maps, plans and elevations that will need drawing. A supply of large sheets of centimetred graph paper is an important aid should you be drawing up your own plans. The exact form this drawing will take will depend on which method you chose to survey your site, and you and the children will have to consider the problem of scale.

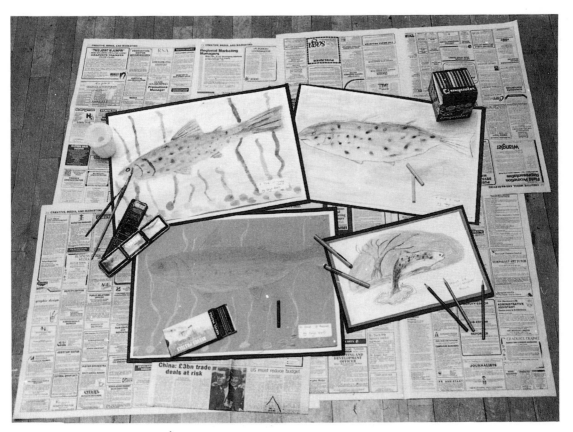

Figure 7.2 *The same image can be expressed in a variety of different media*

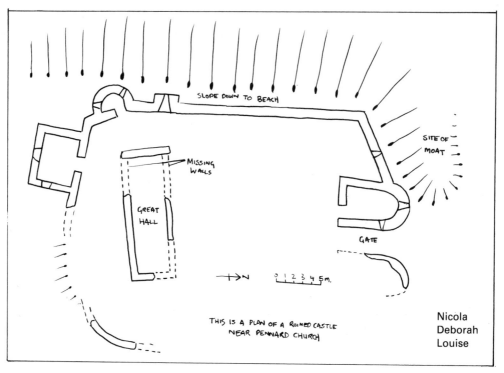

Figure 7.3 *Plans have their own sets of conventions that the children need to learn*

Once the children have drawn out the outlines of their plan they will need to give some thought to the graphic images they are going to use to represent individual features. They may choose to show the scene as naturalistically as possible, a real 'bird's eye view', alternatively they might come up with their own invented signs for particular features. However, at some stage it is worthwhile introducing them to the normally accepted conventions as are to be found on architectural drawings.

These conventions are mainly concerned with the ways in which walls and openings through them are shown, and how changes in relief, associated with banks and ditches are shown. It is normal practice to draw plans of buildings as if they had been sliced through a metre or so above the ground, so that both doors and windows can be shown. If the surveyor wishes to avoid the complications of a large scale contour map he or she will use patterns of hachures, a form of shading, to show where slopes occur.

Sometimes it is necessary to take an existing map or plan and enlarge it, perhaps as a first step in making a model. This can be done in a number of ways: a pantograph can be used to redraw an image often to a known degree of enlargement; alternatively a grid can be superimposed over the plan and the details redrawn on to a much larger grid; or finally, if you have access to an overhead projector you could have the plan traced and then project a magnified version on to paper pinned to the wall and so redraw it.

One of the best ways to really understand a structure is to make a model of it. Models in the classroom can vary from the impressionistic made from little more than junk, to the precise, built carefully from accurately cut sections of card. The model may be free standing and portray a red deer, an aeroplane, a whale, a viking ship or a medieval knight, in which case you will either have to build it as a free standing structure or it could be partially supported by being constructed against a wall. Do consider the

84

benefits of making your models on a generous scale, life-size if possible.

The children may want to put together a model which shows some facet of the landscape, often this will be a building or collection of buildings. The starting point for this second type of model is a strong base made from thick cardboard, hardboard or even wood – old doors make very good foundations for more ambitious models. On to that you will need to draw a plan, it may be to show where the walls and towers of the castle are to go, the location of a village's streets and buildings or the outline of a pond.

Most constructions of this type will need some kind of relief modelling which can be achieved with cardboard boxes, papier-mâché, chicken wire and newspaper, or material soaked in plaster of Paris. It is often best to erect any walls directly on to the baseboard and build up the relief around them. A good way to produce smaller buildings, perhaps for a village scene, is to adapt a standard net to cut and fold to size. Quite complex structures can be made with a combination of smaller units. Larger models will begin to suffer from a variety of structural problems, you may find it best to cut each wall from a large sheet of thick card and secure it to a wooden frame.

Care will need to be taken with the painting of card models, too much water in the paint and the card will warp and the whole thing pull apart. You can either paint each piece in advance and press it – use an acrylic paint, mix your own colour with a little water and some PVA adhesive – or paint on to paper, and glue the paper on to the model. If you want a really professional finish there are a number of companies who market papers pre-printed with architectural textures such as brick or tile. While you are away, you may also pick up commercially-produced models printed on flat card and ready to cut out and assemble, like the Eduprint series on British Cathedrals. These can be good starting points for children interested in construction methods but they are generally on too small a scale to make much impact in the classroom.

Figure 7.4 *Technology plays its part in the construction of large models*

Music and drama

Just as music and drama can be used while you are away as an aid to interpretation and understanding, so can they be used to communicate some of the things the children have discovered once you have returned. The children may want to develop a series of short plays centred around incidents in the life of one of the individuals they have encountered, or similarly attempt to reconstruct the daily life of a group of people. The children may wish to formalise these explorations of character and incident into a play for others to share. Indeed if the scale of the subject was large enough this could become the main vehicle for your follow-up with children researching costumes, building props and devising scenery with a view to mounting a production for the rest of the school and the parents to watch.

There are other 'theatrical' type events which could be worked on during the post-visit period. As an alternative to live action the children may enjoy using puppets to relate some incident they encountered while away. They could put together a programme of words and music to accompany a cine-film or slide show. Some of the thoughts and feelings they registered in the heart of a forest or by the side of a lake could be reworked into a musical composition, again either for their own satisfaction or for a wider audience.

Presentation and publication

I always feel that a project on the scale of a field week, with all the effort and energy that is poured into it, ought to come to some kind of memorable conclusion so that everybody's contributions can be recognised and acknowledged and the school 'community' as a whole can celebrate its successful completion. This celebration can take a number of forms but I do think it important that there is a large social element to it so that whether it

is a production or an exhibition there is a chance for pupils, parents and friends to enjoy the experience of being together at the culmination of a shared enterprise.

We normally try to collect all the children's work together into some kind of bound form which they can then keep as a record of their visit. This can range from a folder, to a loose-leaf binder, to a sugar paper 'scrap-book' into which work is stuck. Perhaps the most permanent and impressive form that this can take is the hard-backed sewn book where the children's work on individual A4 sheets is sewn together, then stuck between card book boards with a suitably decorated cover. These books do take quite a while to make well, so do allow plenty of time for this final stage in the follow-up.

You may find that an appropriate format for your finished work is a publication of some kind to which all the children have contributed and which can be released, both to parents and also interested parties back at the scene of your investigations. This may take the form of a booklet detailing the history of a particular site, a leaflet which can be used to guide other school parties around a nature reserve or a print-out of a computer database recording all the gravestones in a churchyard. You may even have some surplus stock which you can sell!

If you have plans to exhibit some of the children's work you may find it convenient to photocopy individual handwritten sheets for display so that the originals can stay with their authors. You will probably need more in the way of display space than you usually use, so you may have to take over additional space, the hall for example or use something like rolls of corrugated card on which to pin work. When we lay on an exhibition we always try to concentrate on recreating as much of the atmosphere we experienced as possible. This means not only mounting and displaying artwork and models but attempting to 'build' a suitable environment within the classroom. This may be a stone-age tomb through which visitors have to crawl or an underwater scene through which visitors 'swim' by pushing aside the fronds of weed and creatures that

Figure 7.5 *Sewn books produced by children*

are suspended from the ceiling. You may want to play tapes of appropriate music or sounds and create special effects with lighting. Sometimes it is possible to cook and serve food that fits with the theme you have been developing through your display. On occasions we have found that a catalogue is a useful way to sum up the achievements of the children whilst giving some account of who has been responsible for what. Good publicity for schools is always worth having so we have sometimes invited the local press to cover our exhibition.

The kinds of productions mentioned above could be mounted independently or in conjuction with an exhibition so that you are not only looking back over the previous months of achievement but are hopefully looking forward to the next trip away.

Appendix A: Case Studies

A day trip to Oxford

We had chosen to spend some time studying education itself and to this end had visited a variety of other educational establishments in the town. Towards the end of the term we decided to visit Oxford to see how it had been shaped by the presence of the university and to contrast elements of undergraduate life with the children's own learning experiences. The group consisted of approximately sixty children aged from seven to eleven. They were taught by two teachers in a cooperative open-plan double unit. Much of the material is anecdotal but will, I hope, indicate those points where good planning is essential as

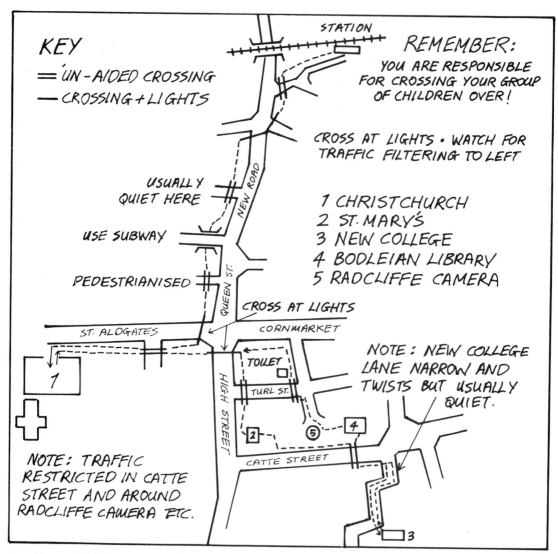

Figure A.1 *The route around Oxford was carefully worked out to avoid crossing too many busy roads*

well as giving a few ideas about the unexpected things which are bound to occur.

We visited the city one day during half-term, and as tourism is a major feature of the Oxford scene it was not difficult to obtain information about what could be seen and how to get in. We quickly drew up a shortlist of sites to visit: the cathedral and dining room and cloister of Christchurch College to illustrate the links between the early university and the Church as well as to illustrate something of the setting for aspects of student life; the Bodleian Library to take in the academic aspects of study in Oxford; the tower of St Mary's Church for the overall view; and New College Chapel and gardens together with the city wall.

As we were a school within the diocese the authorities at the cathedral were most welcoming, they waived all entry charges and let us in through the front gate rather than sending us around the back with the tourists. The courtyard of the Bodleian with its doors still labelled with the Latin names of the different academic disciplines was open anyway, admission to the Divinity School was also free but we informed the desk staff of our intention to visit with a group of children and discussed dates. There was a small charge to climb St Mary's tower so we made enquires to determine how much it was and if there was any group or educational discount. Finally, we called on the porter at New College who was most helpful in discussing arrangements to bring the children along. Armed with all this information and an extensive collection of guidebooks, maps and postcards we returned to Banbury.

As cost was not going to be a primary consideration we decided to explore the possibilities of making the journey by train. Although taking a coach would have been cheaper we thought that arriving by train might be a more suitable way to reach Oxford. Of course, train journeys with large groups of children have their drawbacks. Whereas the coach could have collected us and returned us to school we had to ask parents to drop their children off at the station first thing in the morning, and use staff cars to ferry down any of those who were stuck for transport. Once everyone had arrived on the platform (we had bought the tickets in advance) we took stock. We had with us fifty-two children, and the two teachers had carefully selected groups of eight each and there were five parents and one classroom assistant with six in each of their groups. We had organised it so that although we would sit as close together as possible on the train, each adult was responsible for seeing their charges on and off the train. The other great unknown about train journeys is of course the timing. On the outward bound journey this was not such a problem, but we had organised an elaborate scheme such that if the return train was delayed we would telephone our headteacher who would send messages home with other children at the end of the day as to our estimated new time of arrival. As it happened all went well with British Rail, our downfall was to be in the public toilets of the city.

Our main problem was to be in actually getting around the city. We had gone over our routes quite carefully so as to minimise the number of road crossings and had used controlled crossings whenever possible, but even so there were a couple of occasions when one of us had to hold up the traffic whilst all the children crossed over. The work in and around the different parts of the university went well; the children sketched various buildings, discussed what dining in a great hall would be like and compared this with their own school dining-room, and paced out the sides of the great cloisters amongst other things. Three incidents however stand out. The first was on the grass outside the Radcliffe Camera, the great rotunda that houses part of the library. While a couple of groups took their turns to climb the church tower the remainder sat on the grass with instructions to look carefully at the academic dress that the students were wearing and to sketch it if they could. A number of startled undergraduates found themselves under close scrutiny from thirty odd pairs of eyes and hurried away, their normal calm slightly ruffled; one must always be aware of the effect of the observer on the observed! We took lunch in Christchurch meadows down by one of the many meanderings of the Isis. The children lined the shady banks looking for somewhere cool and comfortable to sit to eat their sandwiches. Unfortunately it was also that time of year when some of the inhabitants of Oxford take to the water on their punts. One group in particular, resplendent in blazers and straw boaters, hove into view. The children, whose only experience of this kind of phenomenum was an advertisement for a certain type of ice-cream that features Italian tenors singing in gondolas, greeted them with a spontaneous chorus of 'Just one cornetto . . .'. The adults just looked away – there are times when to do anything only makes the situation worse. Despite this hilarity the day ended on a sad note. We had earmarked some public toilets next to Oxford's covered market as our final stop before returning to the train. We had not perhaps been as efficient in our inspection as we could have been, because one of the girls found that the lock had jammed. She panicked and had tried to climb over the top of the door, and in doing so had fallen and hurt her ankle. By that time one of the mum's who had been with us had managed to get the door open and all seemed to be well. We examined the girl, and she assured us that although her ankle was a little tender she could manage the walk back perfectly well. However, the next day, after her parents had taken her to the doctor, we were sent an angry note demanding what had we been playing at to make their daughter walk around Oxford with a broken ankle! They were right to be incensed but it was difficult to see what more could have been done.

A week in Whitby

In order to illustrate some of the additional points raised by taking on the organisation of a full week away, I am including an account of some aspects of a trip to Whitby. This actually took place some years ago and proved to be an experience from which all of the staff involved learned several important lessons!

We had decided to organise a field week in the Whitby area because of its contrast with the Oxfordshire town from which the children came. We were attracted by the variety of different landscapes available for exploration and intended to base our term's work on a study of the relationships between land form and land use and settlement. From an examination of the Ordnance Survey 1:50 000 map of Whitby and its surroundings this provisional programme was drawn up in response to our curricular aims and practical needs.

One day in Whitby Town.
One day on the coast.
One day on the moors.
One day in a wooded valley.
One day coach trip to . . . ?

Following a call made on a headteacher who had just returned, and our own preliminary visit in early January, further details were filled in:

Day One – First part of morning in Whitby then walk south along the coast to Saltwick Nab for lunch, walking back along the cliff top in the afternoon. For our children the most exciting single feature of the week was bound to be the sea so we decided to get the week off to a flying start by looking at Whitby to 'set the scene' then to explore the coast and study how the land had been put together by looking at the rocks and fossils. The fisherman we stayed with for bed and breakfast was able to take us out and show us the best route. From the tide tables we had obtained locally, we knew we could not afford to dawdle during the first part of our coast walk.

Day Two – West Beck and Wheeldale Moor. As this was going to be a bank holiday we decided to avoid the coast and town and head for the North York Moors. We thought a whole day on the moors would be too strenuous for our party so we decided, on the recommendation of the headteacher we had

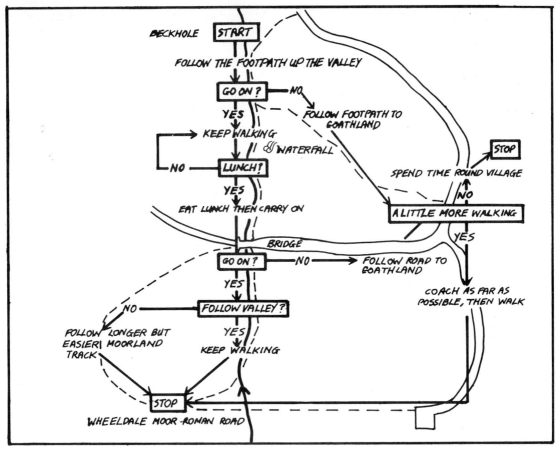

Figure A.2 *Several options were available to us once we set out on our walk*

spoken with, to combine a walk up a wooded valley with a stretch of moorland that was crossed by a well-preserved stretch of Roman Road. We had a number of options as illustrated in the flow chart. This measure created a 'spare' day for us.

Day Three – Whitby Museum, Abbey and Parish Church. All three visits had to be booked, and by putting them all on one day we gave ourselves the freedom to change the programme for other days at short notice if circumstances dictated. We were aware by this time that the riches of Whitby and its people could not be fairly sampled by one full day's visit alone, so we opted to use up our day in hand by returning there the following day.

Day Four – The harbour, fish market and lifeboat museum, hotels and fishermen's

cottages. We were becoming so fascinated by the way of life of the local people that we moved away slightly from our preoccupation with the landscape to take in more 'human interest'. As this was to be the penultimate day we decided to set aside some time for the children to go shopping for mementoes and presents.

Day Five – Robin Hood's Bay. Despite being urged by the owner of the study centre to use our coach on a trip to York or the Captain Cook Museum at Aydon, we preferred to keep our travelling, whilst away, to a minimum. Having experienced some of the excitement of the coast at first-hand, we made up our minds to devote the children's final day to following up some of the issues raised earlier in the week by heading down to the sea once more. This time, however, we thought that one of the nearby fishing villages would afford the opportunities we wanted whilst also offering a change of scene. Having visited Staithes to the north of Whitby and having heard a lot about Robin Hood's Bay to the south, we decided on the latter, a poor choice as it turned out as the place was overrun with other school parties.

There was an interval of some two months, encompassing the preliminary visit, between formulating our outline programme and publishing a final itinerary for circulation to children, parents and other interested persons such as the relevant advisory staff. Even then, we still had a separate set of plans for use in the event of consistently bad weather which involved some rearrangement of items on the main programme and taking up options to visit a local boat building yard, a large hotel and a convent.

Our party was made up of thirty-eight top juniors from two town schools. By a certain amount of rearranging of classes and cover by headteachers we were able to release three teachers. In addition, we took one ancillary helper, one special needs support teacher and two students. On reflection there were two particular days which stick in the memory:

We successfully completed our coastal walk except in one important respect. Although we had walked along some of the beach we had returned the way we had come rather than climb on to Saltwick Nab and come back along the cliff top. When we came to walk it with the children all went well until the time came for us to leave the beach at the far end. The rocks were slippy with rain and there only seemed to be one practical path up them. One of the first children to go on to the rocks fell and badly gashed his lip and set his nose bleeding. The child was not badly hurt but was obviously very distressed. Blood was splashed liberally everywhere, the rest of the party was standing below viewing the climb and the tide was coming in behind us! Fortunately we had plenty of time and adult support to take care of the injury and to slowly bring the party, one at a time, off the beach and get them settled down for lunch.

Later in the week we visited the lifeboat station and great excitement was caused when the maroon went off to launch the in-shore lifeboat. Naturally we enquired about the nature of the emergency only to be told that it had gone out to rescue a party of geology students and their tutor who had attempted the same walk as we had but had been cut off by the tide. As news of this spread the children lined the quayside to watch the rescued party return to land. The locals were not amused and one old lady grabbed the RNLI collecting tin and shook it under each of their noses as they mounted the steps from the lifeboat!

We had a second near brush with disaster during our visit to the moors. After dropping us off at Beckhole our coach returned to a pre-arranged spot in the village of Goathland to wait for us. The first part of the walk up West Beck had one main escape route although others were possible. Despite the fact that it rained during the morning we decided to press on to the waterfall at Mallyam Spout and then carry on up the valley. We had mistakenly relied on reports about the walk from people who had only done it in very dry conditions and we found the second stretch difficult and tiring. Although we made fairly good time, allowing for periods to stop and sketch and to take measurements, by the time we stopped for lunch we found that the trek up the valley had worn us out both physically and emotionally. In addition we had no really clear idea of how long it would take us to reach the end of the valley path, even assuming it was still all there.

While the others supervised the children eating their lunch one member of staff went on to see how far it was to the road in case it was necessary to bring the bus down from the village. As it happened, there was not far to go so we decided to follow the road back to Goathland. If it had been drier underfoot we would certainly have considered carrying straight on to the moors and the Roman road. However, once back with the coach everyone brightened up considerably, as did the weather. Instead, then, of spending the afternoon in a leisurely exploration of the village, we chose to take the coach as near as we could to the Roman road and then to walk up on to the moors to examine it. This was just one of the six main alternatives that we selected. On a different day with different children other possibilities could have been followed up within the same basic framework to have provided an equally memorable day.

Appendix B: Example of Local Authority Guidelines on School Outings

EDUCATIONAL VISITS

In recent years there has been a considerable increase in out-of-school activities in many areas of the school curriculum in addition to general fieldwork and it is considered that there is a need at this stage to give further guidance to schools undertaking such activities. This booklet has been prepared to give heads and teachers concerned with the planning, organisation and supervision of out-of-school visits, an indication of the procedures to be followed in order to ensure that the arrangements meet with the approval of the Governing Body and the Authority.

GENERAL

Whilst it is not intended to give specific advice concerning the dates which out-of-school visits should be arranged since these will depend on particular circumstances, it is nevertheless assumed that in the majority of instances activities will be planned to take place during school holiday periods.

Where for good educational reasons it may be appropriate to organise a school visit of some duration during term-time or partly in term-time and partly in a holiday period, it is required that the following details should be made clear at the time that application is made for approval: the nature of the visit, the proposed activities, and why the arrangement is desired. A number of visits overseas being organised by schools are of a recreational nature only and the Authority would expect such visits be undertaken during a holiday period. Visits planned as part of an educational programme, however, would generally be permitted during term-time.

School visits or journeys should be properly planned and executed with clear aims and objectives. The ultimate responsibility that adequate and appropriate arrangements have been made lies with the headteacher but the party leader has immediate responsibility at all times.

It is important that any activity is planned within the ability of the pupils and where appropriate, training should be given to the pupils as part of the preparation. This applies particularly to physical activities. The standard of care expected of teachers is that of a careful parent but this may be greater in view of the number of children for whom responsibility is being assumed.

ADMINISTRATION

All educational or recreational visits involving absence for 24 hours or more should be detailed on the appropriate form – 'Notification of Educational Visit or Recreational Excursion involving Overnight Stay' and should be sent to this Department as soon as preliminary arrangements are known. The completed form is required <u>at least four weeks prior to the proposed visit and in the case of excursions abroad should be submitted at least twelve weeks prior to the date of departure. Visits that might be interpreted as posing any particular hazard should be notified even if they constitute absence for a period of less than 24 hours</u>. In every case the form should be signed and dated by the headteacher.

The parents should also have been fully informed and their written consent obtained by the school. For excursions abroad particular attention is drawn to the <u>Rabies Regulations</u> and the fact that completion of the form 'Danger from Rabies' is required.

A letter of approval to a visit or further questions will normally be sent back as soon as the appropriate form has been received and the details have been checked. A delay in the submission of a reply can be avoided if all sections are completed fully, particularly in relation to the details of activities taking place and the names of the leader and supervisors of the group.

SUPERVISION

Supervisory provision should be appropriate to the number in the group, the age, ability and sex of the pupils, and the activities to be undertaken. Mixed groups should be accompanied by at least one supervisor or leader of each sex. Whilst the ratio of staff to pupils may vary according to the nature of the visit it is generally recognised that the teacher or other adult to pupil ratio should be a minimum of 1:10 for most activities, and particularly on visits overseas, although it may be a little less generous than this on home visits with older more responsible pupils, say up to a 1:15 ratio. Certain hazardous ventures, however, as mentioned previously will require rather greater supervision with fully trained personnel accompanying groups. Reference to this requirement is made in the 'Notification of Visits' form to be submitted prior to the visit taking place.

It is appropriate to mention here that certain activities whilst not requiring a trained supervisor or leader, but which are nevertheless in the category of hazardous ventures, should as a general principle be reckoned to require an adult to pupil ratio of 1:10. Such activities in this category would be skiing excursions, work visits, planned excursions to sporting activities or meetings generally recognised as providing some degree of danger to members of the general public, e.g. motor or motory cycle racing, air displays etc.

The level of supervision should take account of the activites and the ability of accompanying adults who are not teachers to deal with any kind of disciplinary problem that may arise. Accompanying adults should be aware of any pupils with special needs and be able to act appropriately in an emergency. Activities undertaken away from any recognised education base should be supervised by two teachers however many other adults are helping.

FINANCE

It is important that if money is handled in connection with activities then the financial arrangements must conform to rules and regulations of the Authority and should meet the requirements of the School Governing Body policy on charging. All monies should be properly kept and audited.

Costings should take into account any necessary preliminary visits. A separate account should be opened – money should not be paid into any individual personal account. It is important that receipts are issued and obtained and each child should have a record of payments made.

Parents should be fully aware of any costs and procedures relating to deposits, pocket money and arrangements for obtaining foreign currency.

Where commercial firms or travel operators are used it is important to study the conditions of booking and to ensure that the operator is reputable and a member of ABTA.

TRANSPORT

Care should be taken to assess whether a long journey is necessary for a brief visit particularly for young children. If teachers use their own cars they must ensure that they comply with the law and that by carrying pupils they do not invalidate their insurance policy.

Using the school minibus or coach should comply with all relevant regulations and proper maintenance checks should be undertaken before every journey.

INSURANCE: GENERAL

1 The insurance policies that the Authority already holds that cover educational visits are:

Policy	Covers
Employer's Liability	Employee's claim against Employer.
Third Party Liability	County Council against claims made by third parties (including pupils).

NB: In both these policies, the claimant has to prove the negligence of the Authority for a claim to be successful.

Personal Accident	Employees. Capital benefits only (e.g. death, loss of limbs, eyes etc.).
Personal Accident	Teachers on extra curricular activities.

2 For school visits abroad, it is essential that a Youth Parties Travel Insurance is taken out, covering medical expenses, personal effects, personal accident for all members of the group, adults and pupils. This can be obtained from the Royal Insurance Group, who deal with the majority of the Council's insurance requirements, the travel company, or any reputable insurer.

3 For school visits within this country travel insurance is at the discretion of the organisers.

INSURANCE (AS AFFECTING THE TEACHER)

1 Personal

The teacher, in common with all other employed persons, is covered against industrial injuries by the weekly contribution payable during employment.

In addition to the above, all employed persons have a possible claim against their employer if they sustain any bodily injury by accident, or disease arising out of and in the course of employment. But claims can only be substantiated where the injury can be proved to be through negligence of the employer or another employee (Employer's Liability).

The Council's insurance policy is extended to include employees and teachers in voluntary aided schools, i.e. it indemnified the Governors of such schools.

Out of School Activities

In respect of teachers only involved in the supervision of out of school activites provided that such activites are educational in character and take place in Britain or on the continent of Europe.

Indemnity forms

Some schools still require parents to sign forms indemnifying the County Council against all claims by school children arising from accidents on out-of-school activites. The County Council has two policies in respect of third party insurance cover. The effect of these policies is that all claims by a child against the County Council or a teacher arising from authorised out-of-school activities and alleging negligence by a teacher, will be dealt with under the policies. This does not affect any arrangements which headteachers may wish to make to insure the children themselves against accidents and it may be that they would wish to obtain personal cover where children are, for example, engaged in hazardous activities or are away from home for any length of time. Such policies are, of course, for the benefit of the children and the County Council would not be responsible for payment of the premiums. In consequence indemnity forms should not be used.

2 Liability

The County Council has a substantial policy in respect of claims for negligent injury to persons or damage to property (Third Party Liability). Teachers are indemnified as though they were the insured, and all employees, servants, agents and volunteers are similarly covered.

INSURANCE (SCHOLARS AND TEACHERS)

The question of insurance cover for both pupils and teachers has in the past been a matter of some concern to teachers in control of parties, excursions, etc. and with the increase in out-of-school activity the following notes on points of principle may give you some guidance in this area.

1 **What is meant by 'Cover'?**
The Council can only take out insurance protection on individuals or property in which it has an 'insurable interest'. In the context of the school visit this means that the teachers are covered by the Council's personal accident policy (if the teacher suffered an injury the Council would have to pay sick pay and/or be deprived of that teacher's services). The pupils are not covered because they are a third party to the County Council.

2 **Why then do local authorities or their insurers sometimes have to pay out large sums in compensation?**
The Council protects itself by way of a 'Public Liability' policy. This means that if a pupil, or a third party, were injured as a result of the actionable negligence of the Council (or its employees) then the latter would be covered through its policy against the possible consequences of legal action by way of an award of damages and/or costs. It is important to note, however, that the claim of negligence would, if contested, have to be proved by the claimant, and naturally no cover would be offered by any policy in respect of illegal activities.

3 **What happens if a teacher's property is stolen from school?**
The Council do not insure against theft and in any case personal effects are brought into Council premises entirely at owner's risk. It may be added that cover against such losses is often included in an individual's comprehensive household policy. The personal effects do not always have to be in the home to be covered by such a policy and it is often worthwhile to check this point.

4 **What steps then should be taken to protect pupils undertaking a school visit or other activity whether in this country or abroad?**
The parents can make insurance arrangements on behalf of their children, or cover could be arranged by the school or party leader. In any event it would be prudent for such arrangements to be made and details of suitable policies are available at the Education Office. Before any agreements are signed, however, read the 'small print' with particular reference to the limitations as to the extent of the cover available. No policy will give unlimited cover and the sums recoverable under various policies can vary considerably.

5 **What happens if a company receiving a party of visiting children requires the teacher-in-charge to sign an indemnity before entering the premises?**
Don't sign until you are sure that what you are signing doesn't prejudice or diminish the existing protection enjoyed by yourself and your pupils. If an accident occurs through the negligence of the company you may find that you have signed away all your own or your pupils' rights to take

action with their insurers or through the courts. It would be wise to seek advice from the County Treasurer before a visit if such a requirement is insisted on. This usually applies to visits to quarries, industrial premises, military establishments, etc. and it is worth noting that children are prohibited by law from going underground in a mine.

6 It may be added that since so many excursions are undertaken which are of a modest nature it is quite understood that there can be no question of taking out policies in each case. This even applies to independent activities outside the school premises on the part of older, more responsible pupils in secondary schools. It is simply not practicable to insure against every possible risk off the premises any more than on the premises. It is the obligation of the Authority and its employees, however, to ensure that reasonable provision or other safeguards are applied depending on the age and sense of responsibility of the pupils concerned. It is also recommended that before any unusual excursions are undertaken written notification should be given to the parents.

HEALTH ARRANGEMENTS

Children born in the United Kingdom are normally entitled to reciprocal health care arrangements when visiting countries in the EEC. Application forms E111 can be obtained from the Department of Health and Social Security. Early application is essential as these forms, when completed, must be returned to the DHSS prior to the visit taking place. The additional cover offered by the form E111 is appreciated by some group organisers.

As previously indicated all children born in the United Kingdom are entitled to reciprocal health care arrangements but if a child is not born in the United Kingdom then seek advice from the Education Department if you are uncertain.

If a child is not a full British Citizen (there are other types of Britishness i.e. 'British Overseas Citizens', 'British Protected Persons', 'British Subjects' and 'Citizens of British Dependent Territories') and these cannot be easily identified purely by looking at the passport, please seek advice from the Education Department.

It is essential to follow advice if difficulties relating to health care abroad (in the event of accidents) are to be avoided. It is also necessary to adhere to these instructions to avoid potential immigration difficulties for certain pupils when returning to Britain after the visit has taken place.

The key is: Britain is a multi-racial, multi-national country but BE AWARE THAT NOT ALL CHILDREN ARE THE SAME

SAFETY IN OUTDOOR PURSUITS

It should be recognised that good planning and organisation are essential for anticipating and preventing accidents. Teachers should ensure that they are familiar with the local environment to be visited and aware of any hazards that coastal areas may present, particularly unstable cliffs, heavy waves and undertow. Special care should be taken near a river, canal or lake where a child's swimming ability in cold water is considerably less than in a heated swimming pool.

Visits to mountainous areas can be potentially hazardous particularly for children unaccustomed to mountains. It is therefore important that advice is sought from experienced and competent persons familiar with the area to ensure the suitability of activities. Activities should take into account the ages and previous experience of children.

Schools using activity centres should ensure that teachers have the overall responsibility for the management of the party as they are best placed to assess the ability of the pupils. The school should also ensure that instruction is undertaken by competent instructors and that equipment is appropriate and safe for the activity to be undertaken.

Where it is intended that supervision in part should be provided by persons other than teachers, then care should be taken to ensure that those persons understand in advance what is expected of them and that they are capable of undertaking this role.

(Printed with the kind permission of Northamptonshire County Council. This publication as well as the two other publications in the series: *Outdoor Education – Resource Handbook* and *Outdoor Education – Curriculum Planning* are available from:

Northampton County Council,
Registry,
Education Department,
Northampton House,
Northampton NN1 2HX.)

Useful Addresses

British Trust for Conservation Volunteers: 36 St Mary's Street, Wallingford, Oxfordshire OX10 0EU.

Civic Trust, Education Group: 17 Carlton House Terrace, London SW14 5AW.

Conservation Trust: National Environmental Education Centre, George Palmer Site, Northumberland Avenue, Reading RG2 7PW.

Council for British Archaeology: 112 Kennington Road, London SE11 6RE.

Council for Environmental Education: School of Education, University of Reading, London Road, Reading RG1 5AQ.

Council for the Protection of Rural England: 4 Hobart Place, London SWIW 0HY.

Countryside Commission: John Dower House, Crescent Place, Cheltenham, Gloucestershire GL50 3RA. (Publications from 19–23 Albert Road, Manchester M19 2EQ.)

Department of the Environment: 2 Marsham Street, London SW1P 3EB.

English Heritage – Education Service: 15–17 Great Marlborough Street, London W1V 1AF.

English Tourist Board: 24 Grosvenor Gardens, London SW1W 0ET.

Geographical Association: 343 Fulwood Road, Sheffield S10 3BP.

Heritage Education Trust: St Mary's College, Strawberry Hill, Twickenham TW1 4SX.

National Farmers Union: Agriculture House, Knightsbridge, London SW1X 7NJ.

National Trust: 36 Queen Anne's Gate, London SW1H 9AS.

Nature Conservancy Council: Northminster House, Peterborough PE1 1UA.

Royal Society for Nature Conservation: The Green, Nettleham, Lincoln LN2 2NR.

Royal Society for the Protection of Birds: The Lodge, Sandy, Bedfordshire SG19 2DL.

Urban Wildlife Group: 131–133 Sherlock Street, Birmingham B5 6NB.

Youth Hostels Association: Trevelyan House, St Albans, Hertfordshire AL1 2DY.

Useful Reading

ASTON, M. (1985) *Interpreting the Landscape*. London: Batsford.

ASTON, M. and BOND, J. C. (1976) *The Landscape of Towns*. London: Dent.

ALLABY, M. (1987) *The Ordnance Survey Outdoor Handbook*. London: Macmillan.

BAALPE (1980) *Safety in Physical Education*. Chester: British Association of Advisers and Lecturers in Physical Education.

BAILEY, K. (1979) *Environment and Community*. London: Heritage Education Group.

BROWN, T. and HUNTER, R. (1975) *The Spur Book of Map and Compass*. Bourne End, Bucks.: Spur Books.

BROWN T. and HUNTER, R. (1976) *The Spur Book of Outdoor First Aid*. Bourne End, Bucks.: Spur Books.

COUNTRYSIDE COMMISSION. (1981) *School Visits to Farms*. Cheltenham: Countryside Commission.

COUNTRYSIDE COMMISSION. (1985) *Out In The Country – Where you can go and what you can do*. Cheltenham: Countryside Commission.

DEPARTMENT OF EDUCATION AND SCIENCE. (1979) *The Environment – Sources of Information for Teachers*. London: HMSO.

DEPARTMENT OF EDUCATION AND SCIENCE. (1986) *Geography from 5 to 16*. London: HMSO.

DEPARTMENT OF EDUCATION AND SCIENCE. (1989) *Environmental Education from 5 to 16*. London: HMSO.

GRESSWELL, P. (1971) *Environment – An Alphabetical Handbook*. London: John Murray.

HOSKINS, W. G. (1955 plus reprints) *The Making of the English Landscape*. London: Hodder and Stoughton.

HUNTER, R. (1979) *The Outdoor Companion*. London: Constable.

MAYS, P. (1985) *Teaching Children Through The Environment*. London: Hodder and Stoughton.

MORGAN, M. (1979) *Historical Sources in Geography*. London: Butterworth.

MUIR, R. (1981) *The Shell Guide to Reading the Landscape*. London: Michael Joseph.

NATIONAL UNION OF TEACHERS (1987) *Beyond The Classroom – Guidance on School Visits and Journeys*. London: National Union of Teachers.

RACKHAM, O. (1976) *Trees and Woodland in the British Landscape*. London: Dent.

RAVENSDALE, J. R. (1985) *History on Your Doorstep*. London: BBC.

ROWLEY, T. (1978) *Villages in the Landscape*. London: Dent.

SAINT JOHN AMBULANCE (1984) *Emergency Aid in Schools*. London: The Order of St John.

SAUVIN, P. (1975) *Looking Around in Town and Country*. London: Franklin Watts.

SCHOOLS COUNCIL (1972) *Environmental Studies Project – Teachers Guide*. London: Hart Davis Educational.

SCHOOLS COUNCIL (1972) *Environmental Studies Project – Case Studies*. London: Hart Davis Educational.

SCHOOLS COUNCIL (1972) *Environmental Studies Project – Starting From Maps*. London: Hart Davis Educational.

SCHOOLS COUNCIL (1972) *Environmental Studies Project – Starting from Rocks*. London: Hart Davis Educational.

SCHOOLS COUNCIL (1972) *Out and About – A Teachers Guide to Safety on Educational Visits*. London: Evans/Methuen Educational.

SCHOOLS COUNCIL (1972) *Pterodactyls and Old Lace – Museums in Education*. London: Evans/Methuen Educational.

SCHOOLS COUNCIL (1973) *Environmental Studies 5–13: the use of historical resources*. London: Evans/Methuen Educational.

SCHOOLS COUNCIL (1974) *Education for the Environment*. London: Longman.

TAYLOR, C. (1975) *Fields in the English Landscape*. London: Dent.

WILSON, J. G. (1985) *Follow The Map – The Ordnance Survey Guide*. London: A & C Black Ltd.

Index